BIG MAGIC for Little Hands

Where there is a magician, there is usually a magical mom.
This book is dedicated to mine.

 Published simultaneously in Canada by Thomas Allen & Son Limited.

Library of Congress Cataloging-in-Publication Data is available.
ISBN 978-0-7611-8009-8

Design by Netta Rabin
Cover design by Raquel Jaramillo
Illustrations by Kyle Hilton

Workman books are available at special discounts when purchased in bulk for premiums and sales promotions as well as for fund-raising or educational use. Special editions or book excerpts can also be created to specification. For details, contact the Special Sales Director at the address below, or send an email to specialmarkets@workman.com.

Workman Publishing Co., Inc.
225 Varick Street
New York, NY 10014-4381
workman.com

Printed in China
First printing October 2014

10 9 8 7 6 5 4 3 2 1

BIG MAGIC for Little Hands

Workman Publishing
New York

Contents

Your First Magical Moment

YOU ARE JUST PAGES AWAY FROM learning some of the greatest secrets in magic, but first, I have a surprise for you, and that surprise happens *right now*. You're about to perform your first magic illusion . . . on yourself! Here we go!

Examine the page in front of you. Look to the left and notice the magician. Do you notice anything unusual? When most kids think of a magician, they think of an adult magician with a moustache and a cape. Not anymore. Now *you* are the magician. And the magician drawn to your left will be your partner in this illusion. Back to her in a minute.

Now look to her right. See the rabbit? That's Harry. You're about to make Harry disappear.

Place this book flat on the table and position your face directly over it. Cover your left eye with your left hand. With your right eye, stare at the magician. Just look directly at the magician and then very slowly move your face toward the book. As you move closer to the drawing of the magician you will discover that, just for a moment, Harry vanishes *right off the page*! Move closer or farther and he reappears. If you look over at him, he comes right back. But in just the right spot, while you look at the magician, the rabbit disappears completely.

CONGRATULATIONS ON YOUR FIRST EFFECT. YOU JUST MADE A RABBIT VANISH AND REAPPEAR!

How does this work?

A better question is, *why* does this work? The answer is science, and that is the solution to many of the magic effects in this book. In the case of Harry, we can blame his disappearance on our eyes' blind spot. Each of our eyes has a blind spot (caused by a lack of light receptors in part of the retina, or lining, of the eye). Imagine that our eyes talk to our brains. This tiny blind spot is the one place that doesn't say anything. When you look straight at the important things, you may not notice the details!

As you're about to learn, the secret of many illusions is often just science or math in disguise. Magic is also about noticing little details that others don't take the time to see or understand—like blind spots. Now that you know that, I think you're ready to be a magician. So let's get started.

Are you ready to learn some magic? I have 25 very cool magic effects to share with you soon. But first there is one page in the book meant for your parents. It's kind of boring, but you should show it to them anyway. (If you do, I promise that they will help you build some of the illusions I explain.) Anyway, meet me on the page *after* that, where I talk about my favorite magician of all time, plus some other cool stuff. I'll be there in a minute.

Introduction

(FOR PARENTS)

SO, YOUR CHILD IS A MAGICIAN. Congratulations! He or she will soon be spending lots of time performing, practicing, or thinking about magic. Guess what? You will, too. You probably never envisioned a career as a magician's assistant, but magic will give you an amazing opportunity to bond with your child. Some of my fondest memories are times spent testing out my newest illusions on Mom, or glancing at Dad from onstage, his camcorder aimed at me, at my first show.

Magic isn't just about memories, either. It is a rewarding, enriching art that gives back whatever one puts in, and for many of us, it's a love affair that lasts a lifetime. Magic provides some important skill sets for your child. He or she will be reading, practicing, problem solving, building props, and interacting with adults and peers, all in pursuit of a good performance. Your child will learn advanced public speaking skills and attain a level of confidence in front of people most adults wished they possessed. Never mind that your dinner parties will have a headlining magician, free of charge.

I believe there to be no finer pastime for a child than magic. It provides invaluable life lessons. Here are some of the biggies.

- **CONFIDENCE:** Magic tricks are projects. Each one involves learning, practicing, polishing, and then performing in front of people. This entire process, once realized, is a huge thrill and instills a sense of real accomplishment. All this leads to increased confidence, both in public speaking and in one's ability to follow through on a project.

- **A HIDDEN TALENT:** Being involved in magic doesn't mean your child will become a professional or skip college to join the circus. Many of the best magicians I know perform only in their spare time, for family and friends. Others have integrated magic into their jobs, using effects to break the ice or complete a sale or relax a jury. My father—a dentist—used magic to calm nervous kids in the dental chair. Magic is a great asset in meeting new people, making friends, and, with practice, sweeping the local talent show circuit.

- **A LOVE FOR READING:** With all the digital distractions these days, it's hard to nurture reading in a child. My parents tried unsuccessfully for years to encourage me to read by telling me I could do it for an hour before bedtime. But it wasn't until I discovered magic that I *wanted* to read. That love of reading has spread to many different subjects, but it started because all of magic's greatest secrets are buried in books, and if you want to be a better magician, you have to crack the books.

- **PUBLIC SPEAKING:** It's the average person's biggest fear. That's right—it ranks above drowning or being struck by lightning. Whether your child aspires to be the next David Copperfield or a lawyer or a teacher or a politician, nearly every job involves speaking in front of other people. Magic is all about public speaking, being improvisational on stage, and adapting to situations as they occur.

Magic hasn't just changed my life—it defines it. Magic is how I make a living. It's where I've met my closest friends. It has taken me around the world, and it is the first and last thing I think about every day. This book marks your first day on the job as a little magician's big assistant. Your child is about to learn some really clever and mysterious illusions—which is to say that you, too, are about to learn some really clever and mysterious illusions. In this book, you'll find that the magic that I've chosen is easy enough for a child but deceptive enough for an adult. Welcome to the show!

MY FAVORITE MAGICIAN OF ALL TIME is a French magician with four names that are hard to pronounce: Jean-Eugène Robert-Houdin (say it like "who-DAH"). He was born in 1805 and sometimes I wish I had been born then, too, just so I could have seen his fantastic show. He could make his son float in the air, see things without looking at them, and make orange trees bloom on command. He started performing magic in 1825, and for me, he was the greatest of all time. But he almost wasn't a magician.

His father was a clockmaker, and young Robert-Houdin was going to be a clockmaker, too, if not for a very lucky mistake: When he was young, Robert-Houdin ordered a book on clock making, but when the package arrived, it was a magic book instead. When he read the magic book he was amazed. The magic effects seemed to leap off the page and into his head, and he knew that he wanted to perform magic. And to think, it all started with a magic book.

Years later, a young American boy named Erik Weisz read a book written by the famous Robert-Houdin. Erik was so amazed by the French magician that he changed his name in tribute: He would perform as Houdini. Yet again, it all started with a magic book.

I know another great story that starts with a magic book: yours! You are holding a powerful collection of secrets. You will learn how to make your younger brother disappear, pull candy out of the air, make a hat appear on a friend's head, and be the star of your next holiday dinner. I have chosen some of my favorite illusions, and I have shared with you every detail you need to know. The good news is that great magic doesn't have to be difficult—it can often be done with stuff you may already have around the house, and almost every effect can be learned in fewer than ten steps.

Along the way, I will also share the real secrets of being a magician. Like, what do you do if an illusion goes wrong? How do you get over stage fright? I will also tell you about some of the great magicians of the past (including the Great Houdini, of course). These guys and girls were like real superheroes, and their lives were as amazing as their illusions.

You are about to become the most amazing kid in your neighborhood. And who knows, you might even become the next master magician. It all starts with this book.

New York City
September 2014

How to Read This BOOK

YOU DON'T NEED any previous experience with magic to read this book. I'll explain everything in easy-to-follow steps. But to make the most of your magic, you do need to know some of the lingo. You know how wizards have magic words they use to cast spells? Think of these terms as magic words.

LEFT HAND AND RIGHT HAND. You have to know your right from your left. So if you forget, just check back to this page and this drawing will help you. Also, I know you know where all your fingers are, but we have to learn them by name: thumb, first finger, second finger, third finger, and fourth finger.

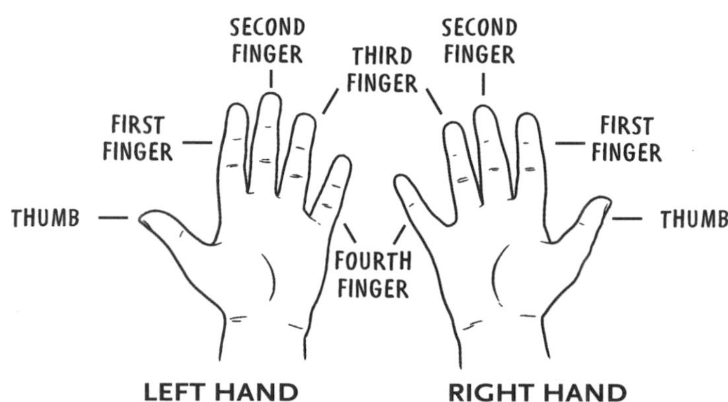

MUSIC. Some of the magic in this book (like the bigger illusions) is better with music. You'll be too busy running, dancing, and crawling to think much about talking to your audience. These effects are marked with a music note. The music you use is up to you, but it should fit the theme.

SCRIPT. Other effects in this book require you to talk with your audience. Some magicians call these words "patter," but let's call it your script. You'll be able to tell the script words from the other words because the script is always in italics, *like this*.

IMPROMPTU!

IMPROMPTU. It's a tough word to spell (and it's worth 17 points on a Scrabble board), but you definitely want to pay attention to the magic labeled "impromptu." Impromptu magic is the kind of magic that you can do anytime, anywhere, with anything. You just borrow the stuff you need and are ready to perform. All the effects that are impromptu are marked at the top of the page as shown so you can easily find the ones you may want to perform right away for someone (after you practice, of course).

RESET. I sometimes refer to the "reset" of an effect. This is how to set it up when you want to perform the effect again. If the reset time for an effect is three minutes, this means it will take you three minutes before the show to get it ready for performance.

MISDIRECTION. This is one of the most important tools in a magician's toolbox. Misdirection is the art of controlling where and what the audience focuses on. You are actually *directing* their focus where you need it.

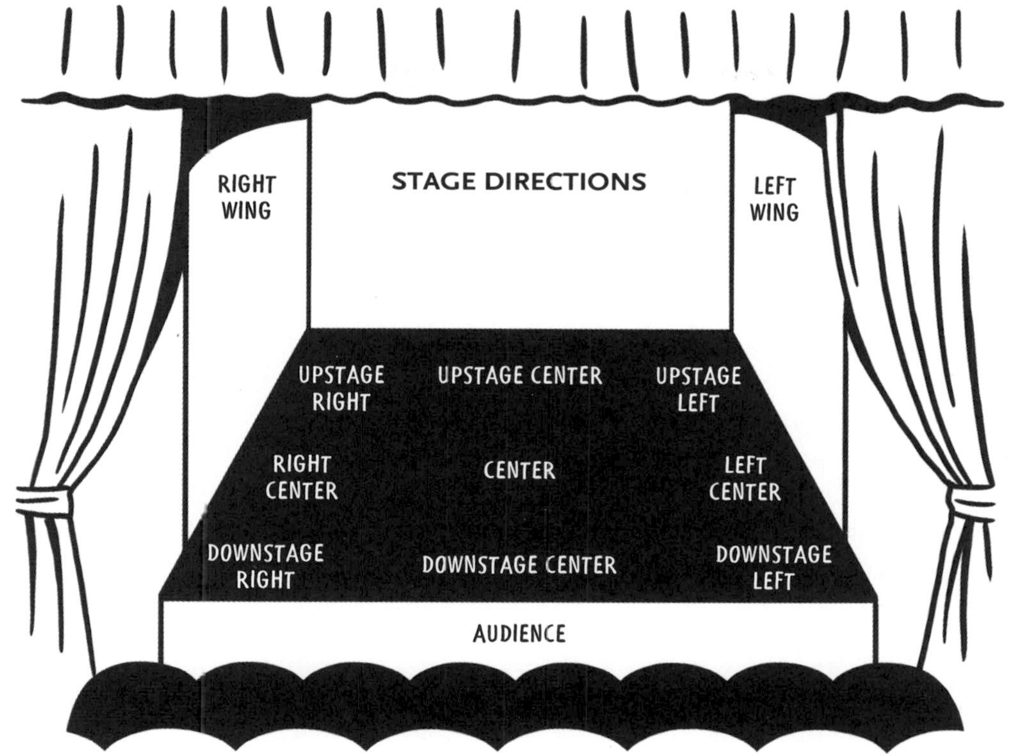

STAGE DIRECTIONS. Because you will be performing the bigger effects in this book on a stage, you should learn the stage directions in the picture above. Notice that all the directions are from the viewpoint of the person on stage. That's just the way it is. For example, stage right is on the audience's left (and the magician's right) side. You can refer back to this map if you forget.

FLASH. This is a bad word in the magic world. If you tell a magician he "flashed," he will be very upset. When we flash, it means we exposed the illusion. If you make a coin disappear but you flash at the end, it means I could see the coin in your hand after it was supposed to be gone. Let's agree right now to practice enough that we don't flash. Deal?

DUCT TAPE. If I have learned one thing in my twenty-five years in magic, it is this: duct tape is the closest thing to real magic. You can use it to build almost any prop in this book, or to repair any prop that might break just before a performance. If you love magic, do yourself a favor and acquire a roll of duct tape.

GAFF. A gaff is an object that looks normal but actually does something tricky. For example, on page 50, you will learn to make and perform with the Breakaway Box. This looks like a normal cereal box, but it's really a gaff (and a very cool one, too).

SPECTATOR. In old magic books the spectator is the person helping. But the definition of "spectator" is someone who watches something, and we don't want our helpers watching; we want them helping! Instead, use "participant." The participants participate.

PARTNER. "Partner" is another word for assistant. Assistants get a bad rap for being just pretty girls who dance around between illusions. But, as you are about to learn, partners/assistants often do more work than the magician. They are very talented, and the magic show needs them as much as it needs the magician. The best magicians refer to their assistants as partners, so that's what we will do here.

EFFECT. Use the term "effect," not "trick." Dogs do tricks. Magicians do magic. Or effects. Or illusions. But please, don't call them tricks!

YOU'RE ALMOST READY to be a magician, but wait! There's one more thing to do before you begin. Warning: Do *not* skip this page. It's very, very, very, very important. It's the Magician's Oath.

Magicians have been around since, well, people have been around. Throughout history they have called us shamans, wizards, sorcerers, and, of course, magicians. And the reason magicians have lasted so long is that we keep our secrets to ourselves. A magician never reveals his or her secrets, and now that you're a magician, I have to make sure you won't spoil any of these illusions. Even if it's just a friend or an older brother, you can't tell. When they promise that *they* won't tell anyone, just say, "That's what I promised when I learned the secret, so I just can't tell." Deal?

As much as I would like to take your word for it, I just can't. In fact, you aren't even *allowed* to turn the page until you take the Magician's Oath. Repeat after me, and at the part where it says "your name here," just say your own name. *Don't* actually say "your name here" or the oath doesn't count. If you don't say the Magician's Oath aloud, the older magicians will find out. I don't know how they find out, but trust me, they'll know.

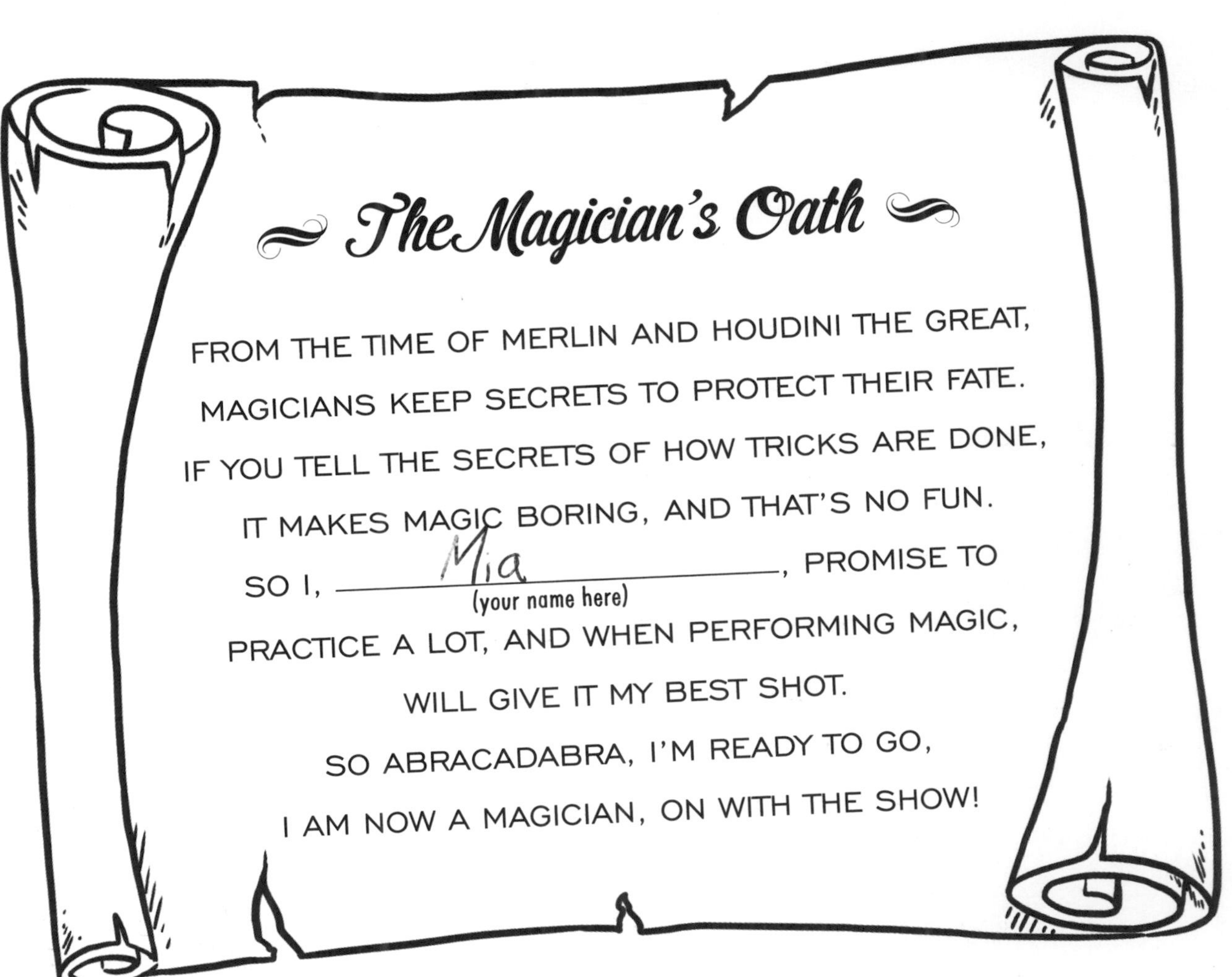

The Magician's Oath

FROM THE TIME OF MERLIN AND HOUDINI THE GREAT,
MAGICIANS KEEP SECRETS TO PROTECT THEIR FATE.
IF YOU TELL THE SECRETS OF HOW TRICKS ARE DONE,
IT MAKES MAGIC BORING, AND THAT'S NO FUN.
SO I, Mia (your name here), PROMISE TO
PRACTICE A LOT, AND WHEN PERFORMING MAGIC,
WILL GIVE IT MY BEST SHOT.
SO ABRACADABRA, I'M READY TO GO,
I AM NOW A MAGICIAN, ON WITH THE SHOW!

~~THE TRICKS~~ EFFECTS

LEVITATING YOUR BROTHER (OR SISTER)

The curtains part to reveal your sibling lying across a table covered with only a sheet. You walk onstage and snap your fingers; your brother or sister instantly falls into a deep sleep. As you wave your hands over his or her body, something spooky starts to happen: your sibling floats a few inches off the table. The audience gasps in amazement.

As you wave your hands higher, he or she floats higher into the air. You outline the area above the body with your finger to show that you use no wires or mirrors. Your sibling mysteriously floats back onto the table and wakes up, unable to remember the levitation he or she just experienced.

HOW IT WORKS

YOUR BROTHER (OR WHOEVER YOUR PARTNER IS) DOESN'T ACTUALLY FLOAT. INSTEAD, YOU CREATE FAKE FEET FOR HIM USING BROOMSTICKS AND AN EXTRA PAIR OF SHOES, AND IT LOOKS LIKE *THOSE LEGS* CAN FLOAT.

What You Need

- TWO BROOMSTICKS
  (or other long poles—ski poles, a mop handle—almost anything long, light, and thin will work)
- A PAIR OF SHOES
  (ideally, your sibling's)
- NEWSPAPER
- A BED
  Note: If you are performing onstage, use a table. I used to perform this one a lot at home, in my bedroom.
- A TRAINED PARTNER
  Younger siblings work well for this, as long as they promise to keep your secret.
- PILLOW AND BEDSHEETS

1 SETUP

Stuff one end of each pole into the pair of shoes. Really wedge it in so each shoe stays in position. Stuff crumpled newspaper into the shoes to help the poles stay in place.

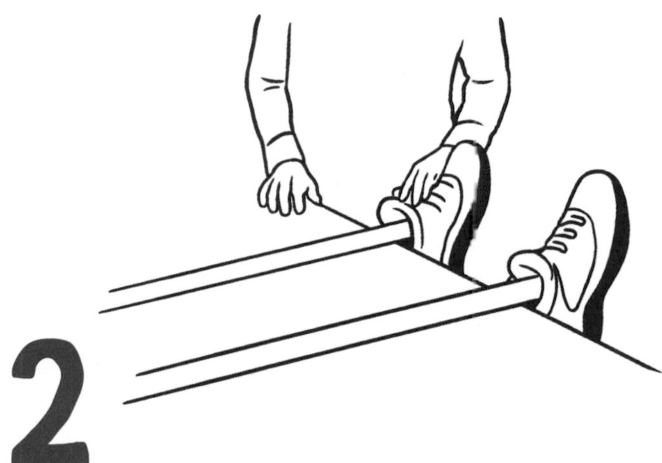

2

Place the poles on the bed or table so the shoes hang over the end slightly. They should be about shoulder width apart.

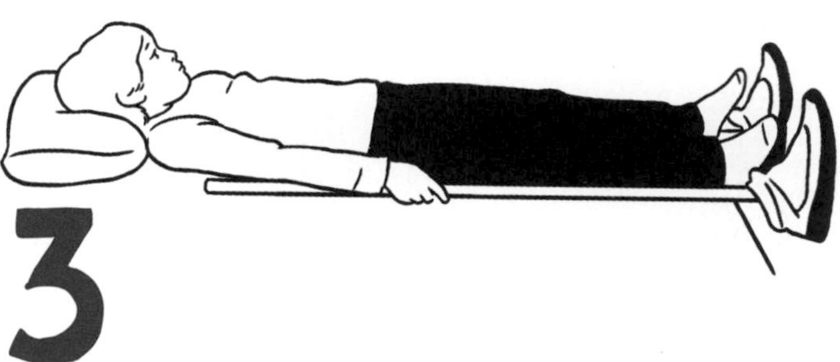

3

Now ask your partner to lie between the poles. Place a pillow under his head. Have him lay his arms along his body, grasping each pole in his hands. His feet should rest on the table, just short of where his shoes will stick out.

SECRET STUFF

Not everyone will perform this illusion onstage. This is also the perfect illusion to prepare in your bedroom. The audience can wait outside until you're ready. If you want to start your performance in front of people, you can hide the shoe-poles under the sheet beforehand and have your audience come into the room after your partner crawls into bed.

Skilled partners can also perform this illusion without a table or bed. You can, instead, angle two cushioned chairs toward each other and ask your partner to lie across them.

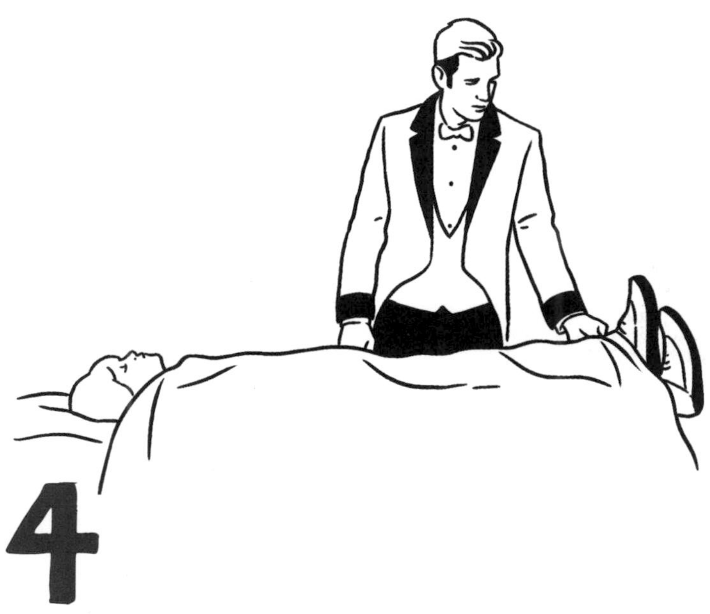

4

Drape a sheet over your partner's body so that only his head and the shoes stick out. The sheet should cover everything below his neck, including his feet (have him point them to mask them beneath the sheet).

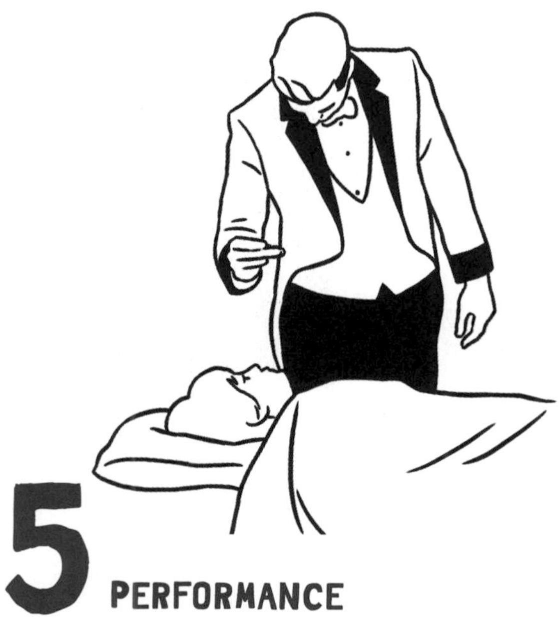

5 PERFORMANCE

As the magician, your role is pure acting: Snap your fingers in front of your partner's face. When your partner sees you snap, he must pretend to fall asleep instantly, in a deep hypnotic trance.

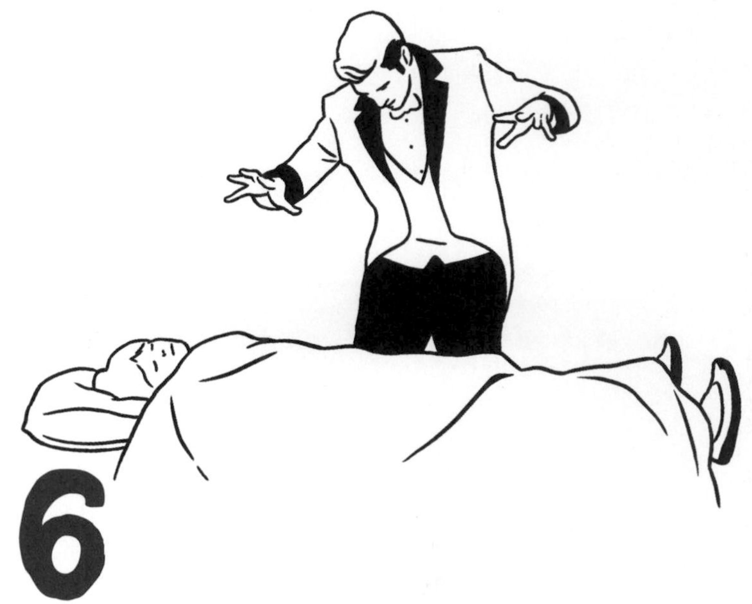

6

Now that your partner is in a deep sleep (he's acting), wave your hands above his body and make large gestures, as if pulling him upward with magnetic powers.

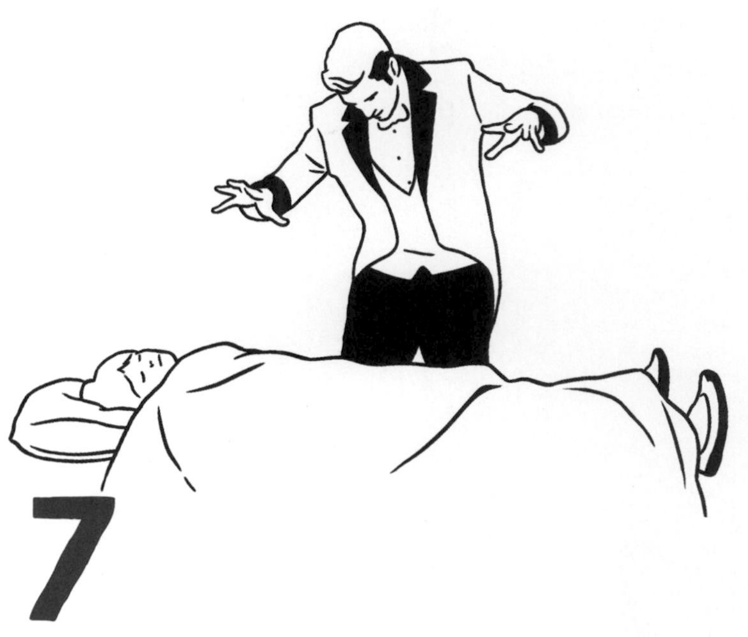

7

As you wave, your partner must very slowly lift the poles off the table. At first, he should raise the poles just a few inches, and it will appear he is hovering over the table.

8

As your gestures get larger, your partner should raise the poles higher. Make sure he keeps the poles even as he raises them. Also make sure he keeps his head tilted back, face relaxed, as if in a trance. The audience will look into his face, imagining what he feels as he floats, and no matter how heavy those poles get, his face must remain relaxed.

9

As you continue to cast your levitation spell, your partner will have to shift positions. Under cover of the sheet, he must sit up and shift the poles under his arms, where he can brace them.

10

Now your partner rocks forward, on his knees, so he can raise the poles even higher. Now it looks like he's floating several *feet* off the bed. Run your hands back and forth above the sheet to prove there are no wires or strings. Just make sure he doesn't levitate too high, or the audience might see his real feet!

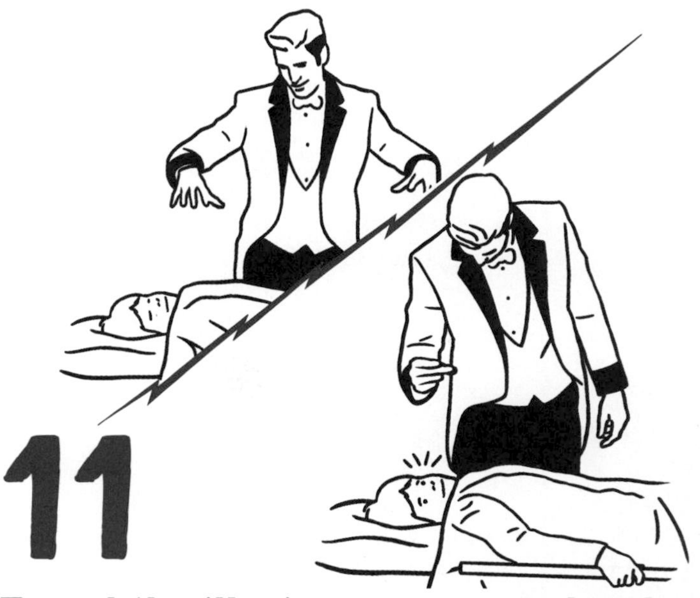

11

To end the illusion, move your hands in a downward motion as your partner lies back down and lowers the poles. Then snap your fingers in front of his face. He should open his eyes and look around as if he has no memory of what just happened. Ask him how he feels. He should simply say, "I feel a little light-headed."

How to Conquer STAGE FRIGHT

DOING THE IMPOSSIBLE can be tough for a magician, but for many of us, the hardest part is keeping cool. A magician has to remember a lot of stuff: how to perform the effect, what to say while performing, and what to do if something goes wrong. Even Houdini got nervous onstage. So how do magicians avoid getting nervous? Here are the four secrets:

1. **REHEARSE.** A lot. In fact, rehearse so much that your magic flows so easily from your fingertips that you don't even have to think about it. Remember that, above all, your audience *wants* to see you do something amazing, which means that they want you to succeed.

2. **HAVE A BACKUP PLAN.** Even if you only plan to perform one effect for someone, always have another one in your pocket. This way, if something does go wrong, you have a surefire, proven effect as a backup.

3. **BE *COMFORTABLE.*** Dress comfortably. If your clothes are too tight or your dress shoes give you blisters, you won't be focused on your magic. Part of being comfortable also means having a familiar face with you. It's often a relief to me to have a parent or friend watching from the wings, smiling.

4. **UNDERSTAND IT'S NORMAL TO BE NERVOUS.** When I first started performing I was always very, very nervous before shows. My dad used to tell me, "It's okay to be nervous. It shows you care about doing a good job." That always made me feel better.

MAGIC PITCHER

In this classic of magic, you present a pitcher full of milk and roll a newspaper into a cone. You carefully pour the milk into the paper cone and then approach the first row of the audience. “In the next few seconds,” you say, “this will either be the greatest magic effect you have ever seen, or you are all going to be very wet.” You then fling the cone open toward the audience. Amazingly, all the milk has vanished and your audience is still dry!

HOW IT WORKS

THERE IS A SECRET JAR INSIDE THE PITCHER THAT ALLOWS YOU TO CONTROL THE LEVEL OF THE LIQUID INSIDE.

What You Need

- ☞ PERMANENT (WATER-RESISTANT) GLUE
- ☞ A CLEAR JAR
  The jar should be as large as possible and still easily fit inside the pitcher. The illustration in step 1 shows the best fit, but as long as you can get close to this, the effect will still work.
- ☞ A CLEAR PLASTIC OR GLASS PITCHER
- ☞ MILK OR DARK-COLORED SODA
- ☞ A SECTION OF A FULL-SIZE NEWSPAPER

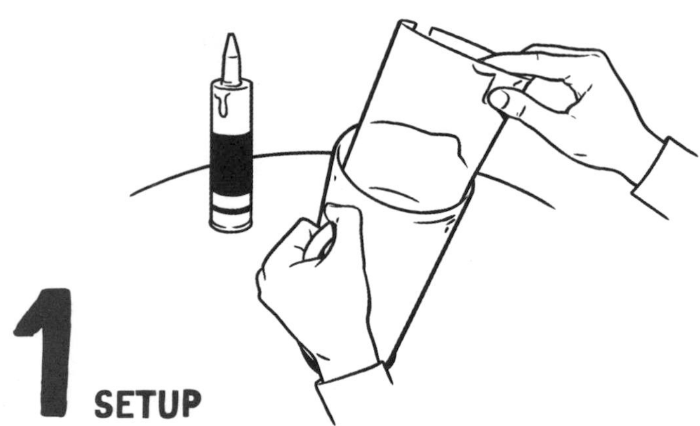

1 SETUP

To create the Magic Pitcher, have a parent help glue the bottom of the jar to the inside of the bottom of the pitcher. Let it dry completely.

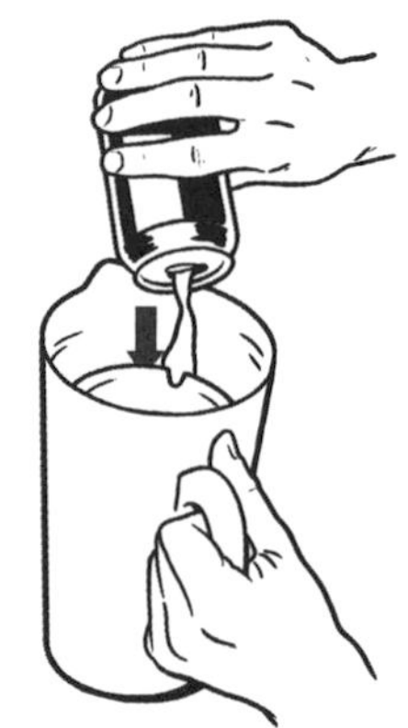

2

To prepare for the show, you need enough milk or dark-colored soda to fill a portion of the pitcher. (And don't drink the liquid after the show. It's for the performance only.) Pour it carefully inside the pitcher but *outside of the jar*. This gives the illusion that the pitcher is full, when in fact you have just filled the narrow space between the pitcher and the jar. Place it on your performance table and you're ready to go.

3 PERFORMANCE

To begin the performance, roll the newspaper into a narrow cone. Fold the point over at the bottom as you say, *"I'll fold this so that nothing leaks out of the bottom."*

4

Pick up the pitcher and pretend to pour the milk into the cone. Actually, by tilting the pitcher down slightly (but not enough to pour anything out), the milk will flow from the pitcher backward into the jar. This will cause the liquid level of the pitcher to go down—and look as if you have poured the liquid into the newspaper.

5

Place the pitcher back on the table. The liquid level is now very low, as if you poured most of it into the newspaper cone. Hold the cone gently, as if you are trying to balance it upright (so you don't "spill" any of the liquid).

SECRET STUFF

This is a great effect to end your show with. It's visual, it's quick, and when you finish, everyone cheers.

6

Say, *"In the next few seconds, this will either be the greatest magic effect you have ever seen, or you're going to be very wet."* Fling the newspaper cone open to show it is empty, and then crumple it into a ball to prove the milk is not hidden somewhere inside. Take a well-deserved bow.

STOPPING WARS WITH MAGIC

You might think magic is just entertainment we watch for fun, but Jean-Eugène Robert-Houdin used magic to stop a war! In 1856 the French government asked Robert-Houdin to travel to Algeria to demonstrate his "magical powers." You see, a local tribe in Algeria was rebelling against their rulers. Robert-Houdin performed an effect he called "The Light and Heavy Chest." He invited the strongest man in the audience to come onstage and examine a very small chest, about the size of a lunchbox. The man easily lifted the chest. Then Robert-Houdin cast a spell on the man (yeah, right!), and said that he would take away all his powers. When the man tried to lift the chest again, he couldn't lift it at all! Robert-Houdin then invited a small child onto the stage, who easily lifted the chest. The tribe of Algerians was afraid of French "magic," and a war was prevented!

So, how did he do it? As I have told you before, the answer is *science*. In 1856, something called electromagnetism was very new and totally unknown to the public. It means just what it sounds like: it's a magnet that you can turn on and off electrically. Turn it on and it's a strong magnet, or flip a switch and it does nothing. Robert-Houdin built an electromagnet into his stage in Algeria. The small chest had a metal bottom. When he wanted to take away someone's power, he turned on the electromagnet under the stage, and the box would stick to the stage floor, no matter who tried to lift it. The idea of taking away powers was just misdirection from the real secret: science in disguise.

KNOT JUST IMAGINATION

You stuff three silk handkerchiefs, one by one, into a clear tube, and then things get interesting: You ask everyone watching to help you tie invisible knots. Then, you invite everyone to throw his or her invisible knots at the silk-stuffed tube. When you remove the handkerchiefs, the impossible has happened: All three handkerchiefs are tied together! That sounds pretty amazing, but in case you needed another reason to learn this effect, here's one: This is my very *favorite* effect to perform for children, and my favorite effect to teach children.

HOW IT WORKS

THE KNOTS AREN'T REALLY KNOTS. INSTEAD, YOU USE TWO VERY SMALL, SECRET RUBBER BANDS, AND IT ONLY *LOOKS* LIKE THE HANDKERCHIEFS ARE TIED TOGETHER.

What You Need

- ☞ BROWN OR BLACK MARKER
- ☞ A CLEAR TUBE
  The best tubes to use are about 1 inch wide and 12 inches long. You can easily make one by borrowing a piece of transparency paper from a classroom and taping it into a tube. If you can't find the material for a clear tube, a paper towel roll will do the trick.
- ☞ TWO ORTHODONTIC BANDS
  If you or a brother or sister has braces, you'll have access to plenty of these. They're teeny, tiny rubber bands. They're so small that you could wear them comfortably as a finger ring. You will need two.
- ☞ THREE SILK HANDKERCHIEFS
  Cut these out of any thin fabric. You need three square shapes, about 10 inches each. I like to use thin red, blue, and yellow silk handkerchiefs. Magicians call these "silks."

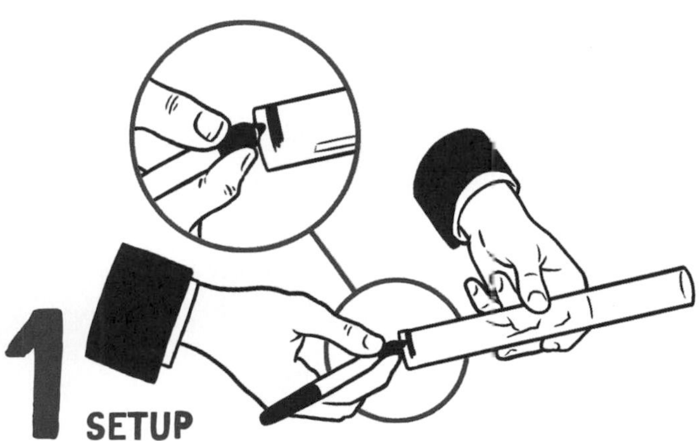

1 SETUP

Color each end of the tube a little less than ½ inch. You can use brown or black for this, and it will look like it's just a decoration, but it's actually done to help hide the rubber bands.

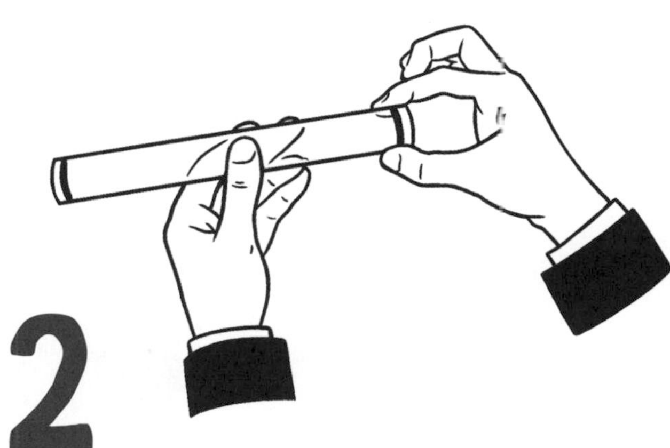

2

Slip one rubber band over each end of the tube so that it blends in with the thin strip you colored at each end. Have the three silks handy, either in a pocket or on a nearby table.

3 PERFORMANCE

Say, *"I have a clear tube and three handkerchiefs. I'm going to place each silk in the tube so that you can see it going inside. I'll start with the red silk. Would you like me to make the red silk magically blow in, or should I just poke it in?"* Your participants will cheer for the first option. But you have some fun with them here: Act as if they shouted the opposite. *"Oh, okay. You want me to just poke it in."*

3: KNOT JUST IMAGINATION

Poke the red silk into the tube on the diagonal so that the corners stick out of both ends of the tube. Ask, *"Would you like me to magically blow in the blue silk, or should I just poke it in?"* Again, no matter what they say, respond, *"Okay, I'll just poke it in. Just like you wanted."* The audience will laugh because you're doing the *opposite* of what they suggest.

Begin to poke the blue silk into the tube.

HIDDEN VIEW

But as you stuff the corner of the blue silk into the tube next to the corner of the red silk, secretly slip the rubber band off the end and around the overlapping corners of the silks.

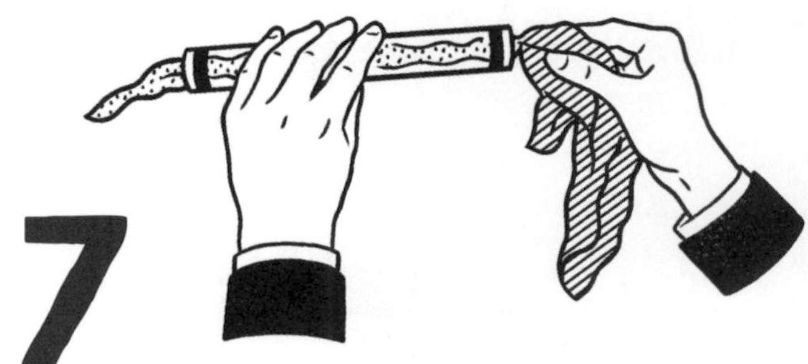

Once the first rubber band is safely around both silk ends, continue stuffing the blue silk into the tube, making sure the red silk stays inside as well. You don't want any cloth sticking out of the ends more than an inch.

HIDDEN VIEW

Do the same silly bit to introduce the final, yellow silk, but flip the tube around so you poke the scarf into the *opposite* end.

HIDDEN VIEW

As before, secretly slide the rubber band off the end of the tube and onto the corners of the blue and yellow silks. Then continue stuffing the yellow silk inside.

10

When you're done stuffing, present the tube so everyone can see it. There should be three bunched-up sections of color: yellow, red, and blue. Then set it on the table.

11

Say, *"Now I need everybody's help—in the front, in the back, the kids, the adults, EVERYONE! Please reach into your brain, like this, and pull out some imaginary rope."* Pretend to pull out an imaginary rope from your ear.

12

"Now tie it in a knot! You can tie a knot like this," you say, pretending to tie a simple knot, like you would tie your shoelaces, *"or you can tie a fancy one like this."* As you talk, pretend to tie the craziest knot a person could tie, wrapping your hands around each other so fast you might just tangle your fingers!

13

Have fun with this next part: Go into the audience and look for the shyest person you can find. *"You see this knot?"* you ask the audience member, taking the imaginary knot from his or her hands. *"This is a great knot. I love this knot."* Now instruct everyone to hold their imaginary knots above their heads, and to throw them toward the tube on the count of three: *"One, two . . . three!"*

For one last bit of fun, the moment after everyone has thrown their imaginary knot toward the tube, reach toward the floor and pretend to pick one up, and then hand it back to any adult in the audience. *"It's okay, not everyone makes it the first time."* This is all just make-believe and fun, but the presentation is what makes this effect my favorite.

14

Make your way back to the table and the tube and say, *"Now let's see how we did. I can either take the handkerchiefs out of the tube or magically blow them out. It's up to you guys."* Everyone will shout for you to "magically blow" them out of the tube. So this time, finally, you agree. Purse your lips and blow really hard into one end of the tube. The silks will pop out all at once into midair.

15

They will fall gracefully and slowly, and everyone will immediately observe they are now tied together. It worked! Catch the chain of silks and thank the audience for a job well done—because, after all, they *did* tie the imaginary knots.

SECRET STUFF

What I love about this effect, by the wonderful magic creator Pavel, is that everyone is involved in making the magic happen. It's one of the few effects you can perform where *everyone* in the audience helps at the same time.

You might be nervous about someone noticing that the silks aren't really tied together. But as long as you show the chain of silks for a moment, take a bow, and then quickly put them away, you have nothing to worry about.

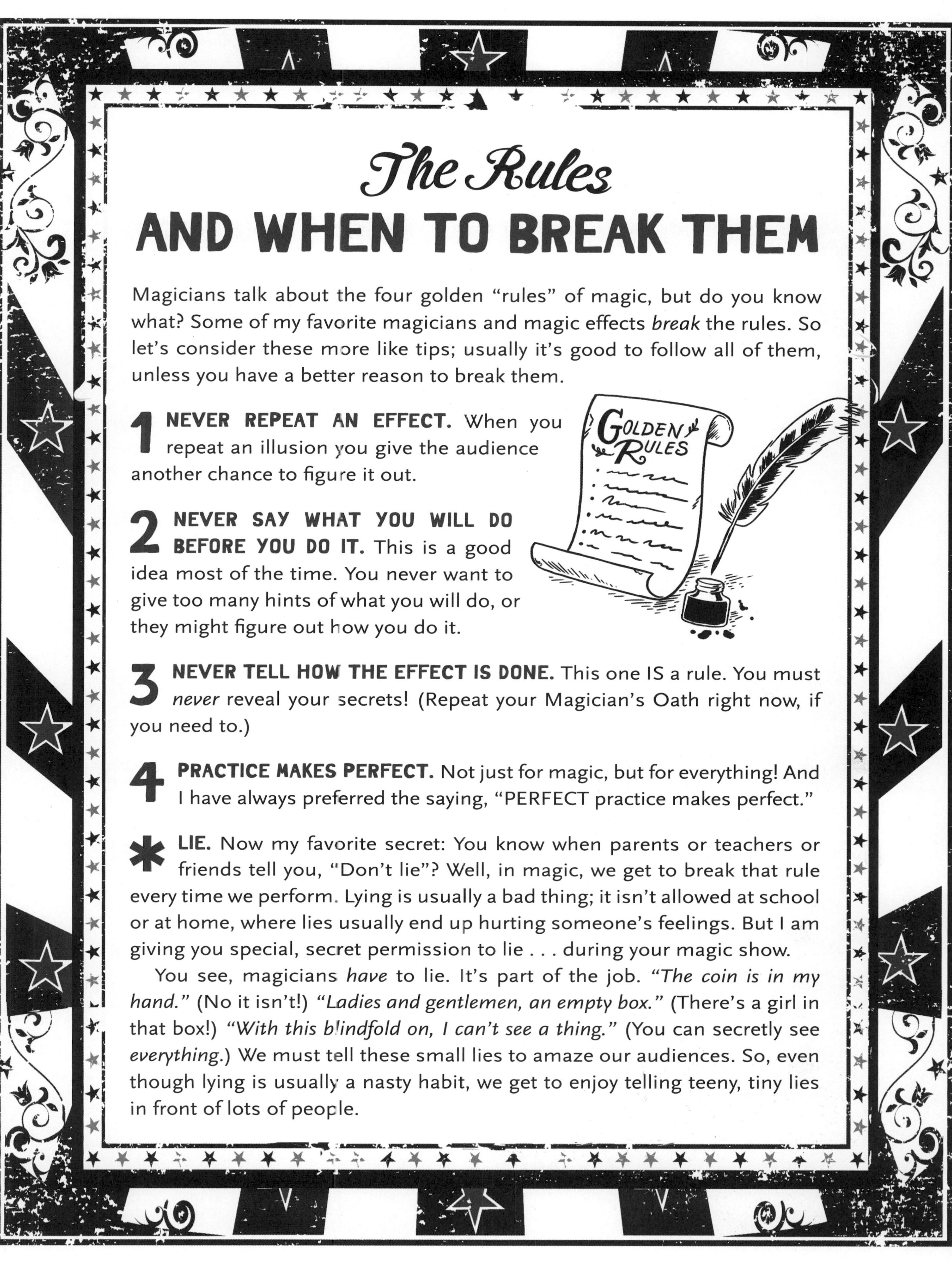

The Rules AND WHEN TO BREAK THEM

Magicians talk about the four golden "rules" of magic, but do you know what? Some of my favorite magicians and magic effects *break* the rules. So let's consider these more like tips; usually it's good to follow all of them, unless you have a better reason to break them.

1 NEVER REPEAT AN EFFECT. When you repeat an illusion you give the audience another chance to figure it out.

2 NEVER SAY WHAT YOU WILL DO BEFORE YOU DO IT. This is a good idea most of the time. You never want to give too many hints of what you will do, or they might figure out how you do it.

3 NEVER TELL HOW THE EFFECT IS DONE. This one IS a rule. You must *never* reveal your secrets! (Repeat your Magician's Oath right now, if you need to.)

4 PRACTICE MAKES PERFECT. Not just for magic, but for everything! And I have always preferred the saying, "PERFECT practice makes perfect."

*** LIE.** Now my favorite secret: You know when parents or teachers or friends tell you, "Don't lie"? Well, in magic, we get to break that rule every time we perform. Lying is usually a bad thing; it isn't allowed at school or at home, where lies usually end up hurting someone's feelings. But I am giving you special, secret permission to lie . . . during your magic show.

You see, magicians *have* to lie. It's part of the job. *"The coin is in my hand."* (No it isn't!) *"Ladies and gentlemen, an empty box."* (There's a girl in that box!) *"With this blindfold on, I can't see a thing."* (You can secretly see *everything*.) We must tell these small lies to amaze our audiences. So, even though lying is usually a nasty habit, we get to enjoy telling teeny, tiny lies in front of lots of people.

HOW TO SCARE THE PANTS OFF YOUR PARENTS

You place one hand on the top of your head and one hand on your chin, and quickly twist your head. The moment you do, the audience hears the bones in your neck crack—an awful sound. But somehow . . . you're just fine.

We're focusing on really amazing magic in this book, but we'll make an exception to include one funny, scary prank, because the gag itself is a kind of illusion. You can try this on your mom or dad right now!

HOW IT WORKS

YOU HAVE A PLASTIC CUP UNDER YOUR ARM THAT, WHEN CRUSHED AGAINST YOUR BODY, SOUNDS REMARKABLY LIKE THE BREAKING OF BONES.

What You Need

☞ A DISPOSABLE PLASTIC CUP
Use the kind that won't shatter when you crush it. Test the sound by closing your eyes and crumpling the cup. If you can imagine bones breaking, you have a winner.

1 SETUP

Place the cup under your left arm. As long as you have a fairly loose-fitting shirt, nobody will notice it. For best results, place the cup *under* your shirt or jacket so it's totally hidden from view.

2 PERFORMANCE

When you're ready to perform, place your right hand on top of your head and your left hand on your chin. Explain that you have a weird pain in your neck.

3

Before anyone can offer to rub it for you, quickly jerk your head to the side as you *pretend* to twist your head between your hands. (Don't *actually* tug at your head with your hands or you could really hurt yourself.)

4

The natural action of pulling your left arm downward as you move your head causes your upper arm to crush the cup against the side of your body. Timed right, this looks *and* sounds perfect.

SECRET STUFF

Use this as a comedy illusion and secretly ditch the cup later. Or, include this in your show. You'll get lots of *ooohs* and *ouches* when you first do it, and if you then reach under your arm and show the crushed cup, you'll get a big laugh. Exposing magic (even for a laugh) isn't a good idea, but this illusion is so basic that it's okay.

IT'S A WRAP

You walk onstage alongside your partner, Dan. You display a large sheet between you onstage. Dan stands against the surface of the sheet, and you wrap him—mummy style—so the audience can see only his outline. When you unwrap Dan a moment later, you reveal that he has changed into his sister Michelle! Where is Dan? You point toward the back of the room. Dan is there, at the back of the theater, blowing a whistle to call attention to his reappearance.

HOW IT WORKS

THIS ONE IS ALL IN THE TIMING OF HOW YOU WRAP THE SHEET. HIS SISTER IS HIDDEN FROM VIEW AND SWITCHED INTO PLACE AS DAN MAKES A SECRET ESCAPE. HE RUNS AROUND TO THE BACK OF THE ROOM FROM OUTSIDE, AND IS REVEALED AT JUST THE RIGHT MOMENT.

What You Need

- **TWO PARTNERS**
  It helps to have helpers/partners who are roughly the same height.
- **A CURTAIN**
  You must perform this illusion directly in front of a curtain that has an opening in the center.
- **A SHEET**
  You need a very large bedsheet that you can't see through, even onstage with a spotlight shining.
- **A WHISTLE**
  It helps to have a whistle or a drum—anything that makes a loud noise.

1 SETUP

This illusion is more like a dance routine than a magic effect; everyone must be light on his feet and smooth in his actions. You will have to practice so that everything flows perfectly.

You begin onstage, stage left. Your male partner, Dan, begins stage right. Position your secret, female partner behind the side curtain.

2 PERFORMANCE

Hold the sheet at the upper corners, stretching it between you and Dan. Make sure that the sheet touches the ground as you display it. (Otherwise, the audience might notice an extra pair of feet that aren't supposed to be there!)

HIDDEN VIEW

3

Now Dan twists behind the sheet and out of audience view. It will appear as if he twists himself into the sheet and toward you, the magician. Actually, as he goes behind the sheet, Michelle quietly steps out from behind her curtain, hidden by the sheet. She pinches the sheet at the same spot Dan is holding it . . .

4

. . . allowing Dan to release the sheet and walk quickly and quietly behind the curtain, offstage. Once Dan is safely offstage . . .

5

. . . Michelle continues to roll herself into the sheet. Make sure the sheet remains touching the floor the entire time.

6

Now you carefully escort her (using small steps—remember, she can't see!) to the center of the stage. While you are doing this, Dan secretly runs around to the front of the theater. He walks through the doors and positions himself near the back of the room, with his whistle at the ready.

7

To reveal that Dan has changed into Michelle, unwrap her. *Ta-da!* Then ask, *"But if Dan has changed places with Michelle, where is Dan?"*

What Should I Do
IF AN EFFECT GOES WRONG?

Doing the impossible can be difficult. If it were easy, it wouldn't be considered impossible! Audiences understand that magic takes incredible skill, preparation, and concentration. And as long as they see that you're trying your best, they will enjoy the show.

I'll share another secret with you: When something goes wrong, just keep going, because you will probably be the only one to notice. You read that correctly—you will probably be the only one who knows there was a mistake. You see, magic effects are like clocks: There are lots of moving parts that nobody can see. Even when one part goes wrong, people usually only notice the parts going right.

8

Then point to the back of the audience. Make sure that whoever is running lights in the theater can angle the spotlight toward Dan, who makes his presence at the back of the theater known by blowing his whistle.

SECRET STUFF

The key to this illusion is that all three of you know your roles and where you're going. This way, everything happens fast and smoothly. And although the magician doesn't have much to do with the illusion, he has *everything* to do with the presentation. It is your gestures, what you say, and where you look that will create the illusion of two people changing magically.

IMPROMPTU!

SPOOK-KEY

You display a beautiful, old metal key to your audience, and place it on your hand. Without you moving a muscle, the "haunted" key mysteriously turns over on its own.

HOW IT WORKS

IN THIS ASTOUNDING ILLUSION, THE WEIGHT AND SHAPE OF CERTAIN ANTIQUE KEYS DOES EVERYTHING FOR YOU. JUST ANGLING YOUR HAND A BIT CAUSES THE KEY TO SEEMINGLY TURN OVER ON ITS OWN.

What You Need

☞ A LARGE, OLD KEY

These are very easy to find at antique shops, garage sales, online, or perhaps in your grandpa's garage. They are often referred to as skeleton or barrel keys. Look for the largest one you can find—the heavier, the better. You also want a key that is round in the middle, like a straw, so that it rolls over easily.

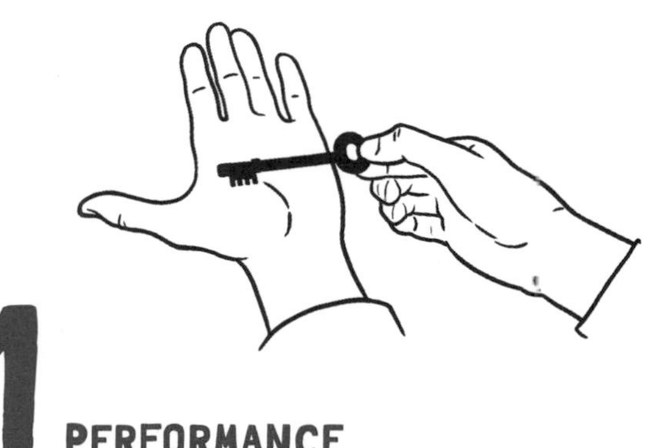

1 PERFORMANCE

"This is a very old key," you say, presenting the key to a participant to examine. *"It was used to lock and unlock doors many years ago. It was turned in its lock so many times that now it turns on its own. I'll show you."*

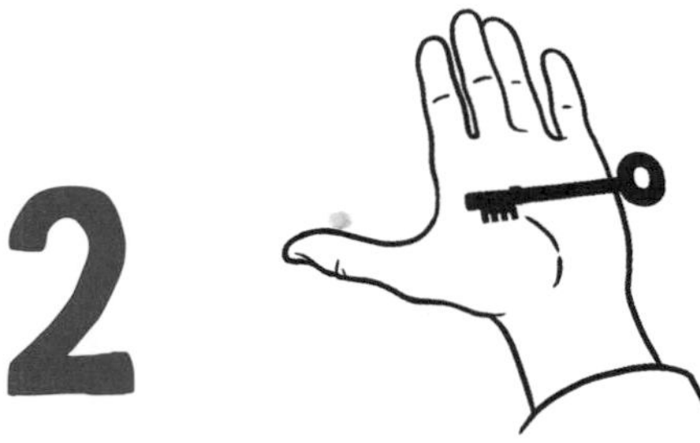

2

Place the key on your upturned left hand so that the end of the key (the bow) hangs off your palm completely.

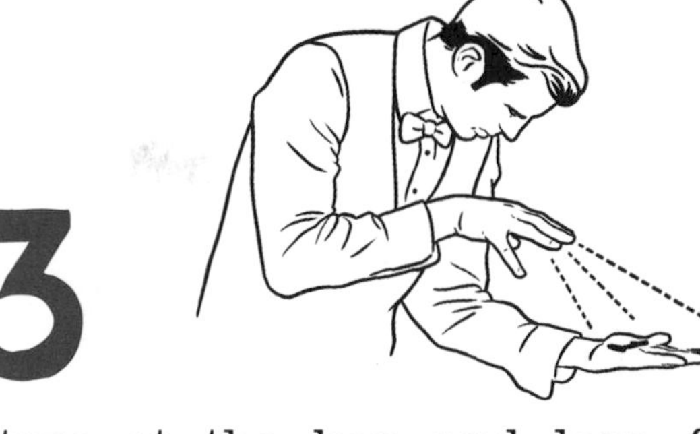

3

Stare at the key and lean forward with your body, as if you believe the key might turn over on its own. As you lean forward, tip your left palm downward very, very, *very* slightly. If the audience can tell that you're tipping your hand forward, the illusion is ruined, so the—ahem—*key* here is subtlety.

4

As you tip your hand forward, the key will slowly start to rotate. Don't break concentration, and don't move. Once the key blade starts to turn, its own weight will finish the job and complete the rotation!

The key will turn slower while the blade is angled upward, and then will turn over all the way in your hand. This is one of the few moments in magic where the magician can observe the magic without so much as moving a muscle!

SECRET STUFF

Don't give up on "Spook-Key" simply because you don't have a key around the house. Chances are good that a neighbor has one he isn't using. And it's worth it when you do find one because you can keep it in your pocket to perform for friends, or for a big group of people, all huddled around you.

VANISHING TEACUP

In this treasured classic of magic, you cause a fragile teacup to vanish completely! This is the perfect effect to perform *with* a parent, because it's (secretly) a team effort.

HOW IT WORKS

IT LOOKS LIKE YOU VANISH A TEACUP FROM UNDER A PAPER NAPKIN. BUT THE TEACUP NEVER ACTUALLY GOES UNDER THE NAPKIN, THANKS TO A SIMPLE GAFF AND SOME HELP FROM A FRIEND.

What You Need

- ☞ PENCIL
- ☞ A TEACUP AND MATCHING SAUCER
  Your mom probably has an old set in her cupboard. Your grandma definitely has an old set in her cupboard. If you don't have one around the house that's okay to glue together, look for an inexpensive one at a secondhand store or yard sale.
- ☞ PIECE OF CARDSTOCK OR THIN CARDBOARD
  A cereal box or old notebook cover works well.
- ☞ SCISSORS
- ☞ GLUE
- ☞ PAPER NAPKIN
- ☞ A TRUSTWORTHY PARTNER
  Parents work great for this.

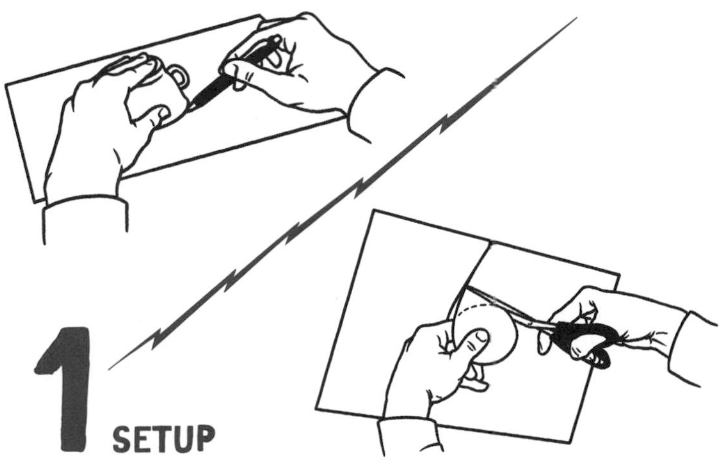

1 SETUP

With a pencil, trace the mouth of the cup onto the cardstock. Use the scissors to cut out the cardstock circle.

2

Glue the base of the teacup to the center of the saucer.

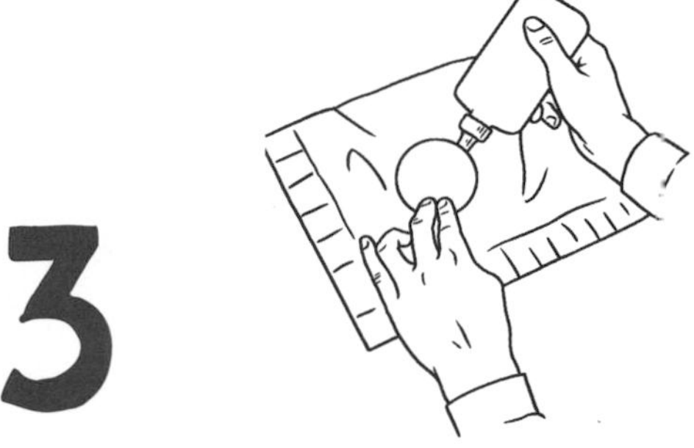

3

Center and glue the round cardboard piece onto the underside of the paper napkin. Now you're ready to perform.

4 PERFORMANCE

Have your partner bring you the cup and saucer. Have her walk toward you slowly, as if the teacup could fall at any moment.

5

Meanwhile, unfold the napkin and display it, without showing the round cutout on the other side. Your partner says, *"I thought you might like some tea before your next effect."*

7: VANISHING TEACUP

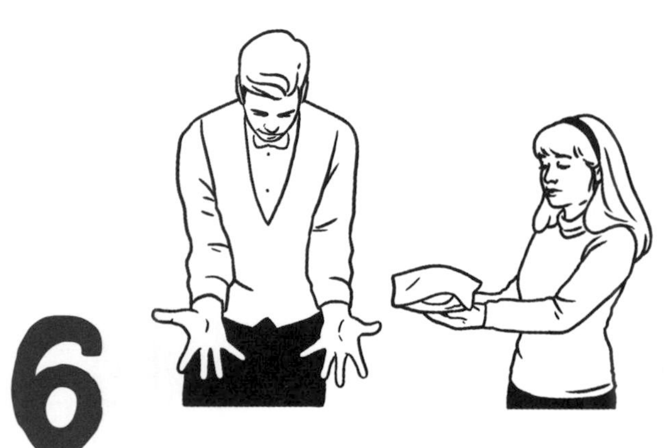

6

As your partner holds the teacup, cover it with the napkin so that the circular cutout is directly above the top of the teacup. Show your hands empty, front and back, and then *pretend* to lift the teacup off the saucer.

7

Actually, you place your right hand above the cup and lift just the circular cutout. At the same time . . .

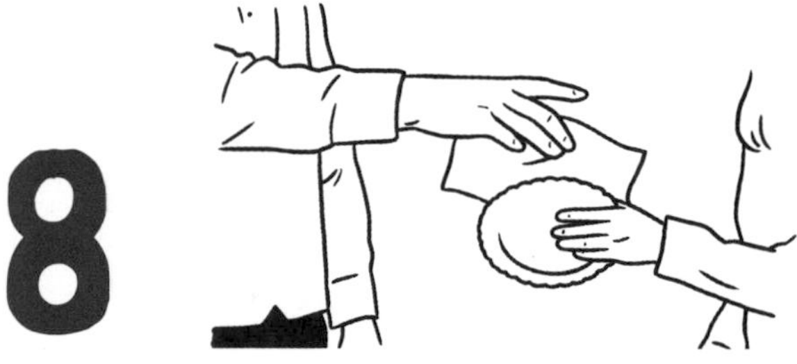

8

. . . your partner turns the plate inward, toward her body, hiding the attached teacup entirely. The audience will only see the bottom of the saucer. She can then walk away or casually place the plate back in your magic case if you have one. Just make sure she doesn't flash the teacup glued to the saucer.

9

From the audience's viewpoint, the napkin you hold looks like it is draped over the teacup. If only they knew . . .

10

You say, *"That's very nice of you, but I'm not thirsty right now."* Then, smash your hands together quickly, crumpling the napkin entirely. Throw it over your shoulder and confidently begin your next effect.

SECRET STUFF

The same method can be used for other vanishes. You could vanish a toy off a tray, or a chess piece off a chessboard. If you can glue it to a flat surface, you can make it disappear!

ROPE ESCAPE

Your partner ties your hands very tightly with a length of rope, yet you escape within seconds. The famous illusionist Harry Houdini was known to perform a spectacular feat very much like this.

HOW IT WORKS

YOUR PARTNER TIES BOTH OF YOUR HANDS TOGETHER IN A SPECIAL WAY THAT LOOKS VERY SECURE BUT IS ACTUALLY QUITE LOOSE.

What You Need

☞ A TRUSTWORTHY PARTNER

☞ A LENGTH OF ROPE (AT LEAST 2 FEET LONG)
Clothesline works well, and in a pinch you could use thick ribbon or a thin strip of cloth.

1 PERFORMANCE

Ask your partner to drape the length of rope over your left wrist.

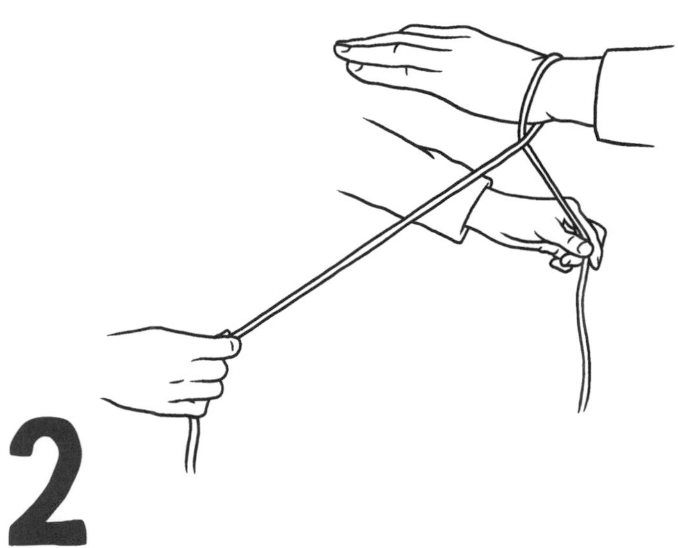

2

Have your partner cross the ends of the rope under your left wrist. (Your left palm should be facing down, so you should see the rope crossed just beneath your left palm.)

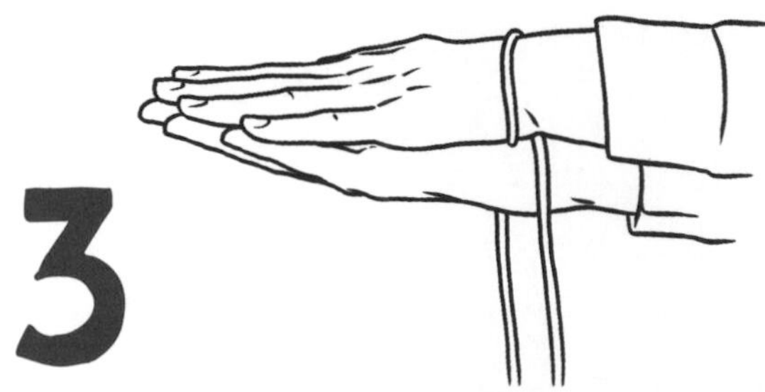

3

Place your right palm against the palm of your left hand so that your wrists line up. Your partner can drop the rope.

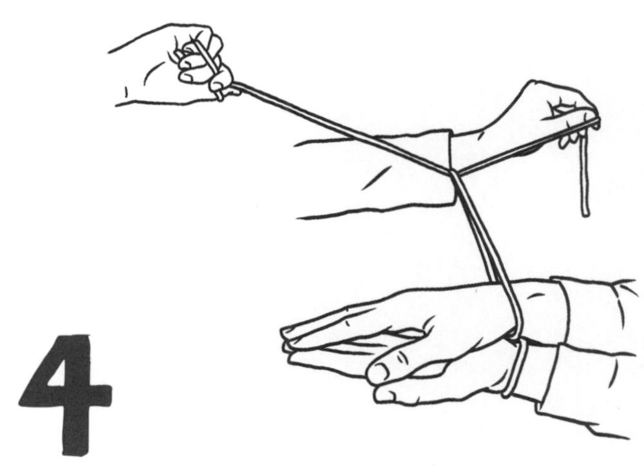

4

Rotate your hands, still clamped, so the right hand is on top. Ask your partner to re-grasp the ends and tie them around your right wrist as tightly as possible: double knot, crazy loop-the-loop, slipknot, whatever. You can even have a volunteer tie the knot. Encourage your helper to tie the knot very tightly—so tightly there would be no way for you to escape.

5

Now borrow someone's jacket and ask your partner to hold it up over your hands so that the secret of your escape will remain out of sight.

HIDDEN VIEW

6

Once your hands are out of sight, simply twist your hands in opposite directions. You will discover that the rope is tied in one big, loose loop that has a twist in it. By untwisting it, the rope loosens and allows you to easily slide one hand out.

7

Slide out your right hand and hold it up, above the jacket. Extend three fingers as you say, *"I will escape from this rope on the count of three."* For a second, people won't realize how silly this is. You just held up your hand and announced when you will escape . . . but you have already escaped!

HIDDEN VIEW

8

Quickly move your hand behind the jacket again, slip it back into the loop of rope the same way you escaped, and re-twist your hand.

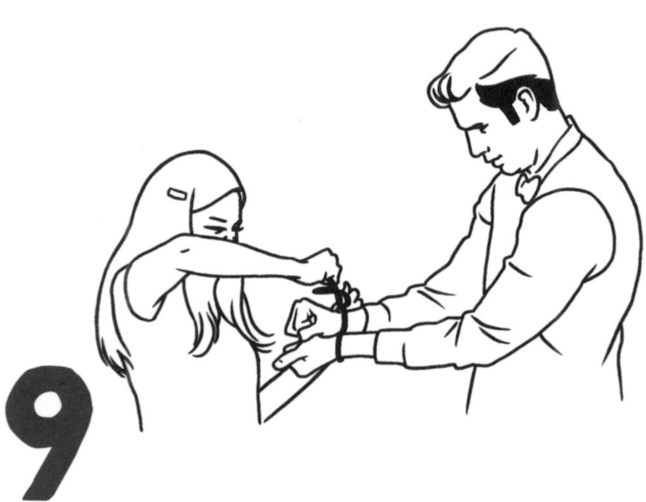

9

Now hold up both hands to show that your hands are still tied tightly. You can even have a volunteer verify the knot is still tight.

10

Place your hands behind the jacket again, slip out as I already showed you, and this time scratch your nose for a moment. Say, *"Sorry, I had an itch, just a minute."* Once again, you have escaped in seconds, for a silly reason. More laughs.

11

Move your hand behind the jacket and slip back into the rope. Then you can once again raise your hands above the level of the jacket to show that your hands are still bound.

12

When you are ready to escape once and for all, move your hands behind the jacket, free both hands, and toss the rope to the floor. Move both hands up above your head, and take a bow.

SECRET STUFF

Escapes are different from magic effects. With magic effects, you demonstrate the impossible. Your audience knows what you're doing isn't real, and that is exactly what makes magic so much fun: It's a game of make-believe between you and the audience. Escapes, on the other hand, are fun because they are real. People know that it's possible to escape from ropes or chains or boxes, but they also know that it's very difficult.

Houdini's

GREAT PLANE ESCAPE

YOU PROBABLY KNOW Houdini as the greatest escape artist who ever lived, made famous by rope escapes like the one you just learned. But did you know he also made silent films?

Once, while Houdini was filming a movie called *The Grim Game,* there was a terrible accident. The scene was supposed to show Houdini climbing, by rope, from one plane to another. But during the filming the two planes collided mid-air, and then both went crashing to the ground. Fortunately, the pilots and Houdini survived. The next day, although a little banged up, Houdini announced that he had survived a terrible plane crash.

But here's my favorite part: It was a lie! A stuntman—not Houdini—was in the air filming that day. Robert Kennedy was the name of the man who *really* had to climb down a rope high in the sky, from one plane to another. When the planes collided, it was Robert Kennedy, *not* Houdini, who survived the crash. It was publicized as Houdini's greatest escape, and Houdini wasn't even in the plane.

THE AMAZING TUBE OF MYSTERY

OR DOOM, OR WHATEVER

You hold up an empty tube and wave to your audience through it—clearly nothing inside. Then, you wave your hand over the tube, and cause silk streamers and candy to appear . . . all from that same empty tube . . . The Amazing Tube of Mystery . . . or Doom . . . or whatever!

HOW IT WORKS

THE TUBE HAS A SECRET COMPARTMENT YOU CAN ONLY SEE FROM ONE SIDE, AND THAT COMPARTMENT IS FILLED WITH THE THINGS YOU WILL PRODUCE.

What You Need

- ☞ TWO PIECES OF POSTER BOARD (12 X 18 INCHES)
  Make sure both pieces are the same color.
- ☞ SCISSORS
- ☞ MASKING OR CLEAR PACKING TAPE
- ☞ MARKER
- ☞ SILK STREAMERS
  You can actually fill the secret compartment with whatever you like: napkins, popcorn, or even candy. If you're using any loose items just make sure you use at least one handkerchief or cloth to pack everything tightly.

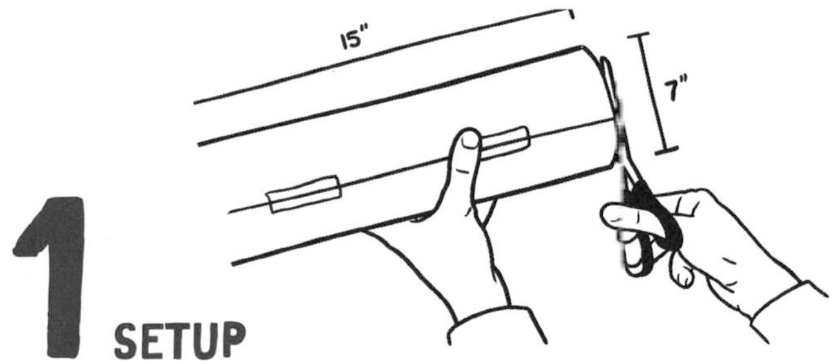

1 SETUP

First make the tube, which is really *two* tubes, one inside the other. For the outer tube, trim the first piece of poster board so you can roll it into a tube about 7 inches wide and 15 inches long. (You can make the tube smaller or wider, depending on how much stuff you want to produce.) Tape the tube along the edge. Trim the second piece of poster board so that it's slightly smaller and more tapered (cone-shaped) than the first: One end of the smaller tube should match the width of the end of the big tube (7 inches), but the other should be about 3 inches across. This is the inner tube. Tape it along the edge.

2

Decorate the outside of the outer tube with a question mark and you have a Tube of Mystery; decorate it with dark colors and you have a Tube of Doom. Decorate the tube however you like, really!

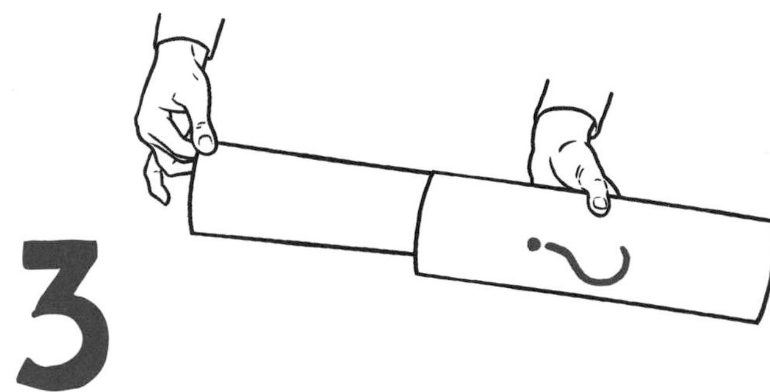

3

Insert the inner, tapered tube into the larger outer tube. Line up the wide ends.

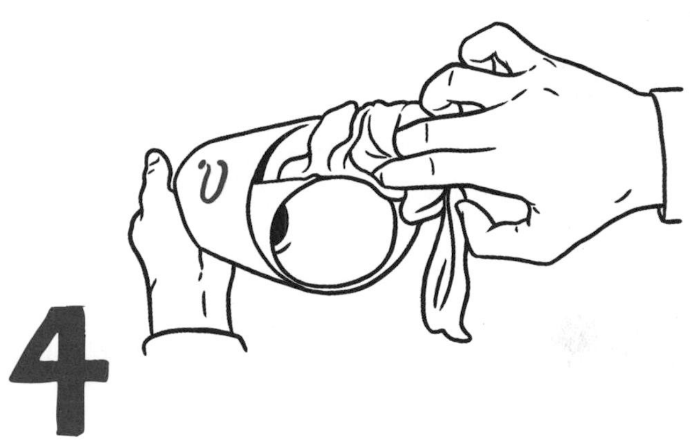

4

Stuff the streamers (or other items you wish to produce) into the space between the two tubes. When I perform this effect, I like to use a bunch of thin silk handkerchiefs tied together at the corners.

HIDDEN VIEW

5

When the tubes are assembled and the streamers are in place, your gaff is ready. When you show the audience the end of the tube, everything looks normal. From your angle, it looks pretty tricky. (Fortunately, you are the only one who sees the tube from this angle.)

6

PERFORMANCE

When you are ready to perform, look through the tube at the audience to show that it's empty. Try to make eye contact with everyone. If you can see the participants looking back at you, you know they can see that the tube is empty. Turn your head left and right, so even the kids on the sides can see.

7

Now hold the tube so the opening is angled straight up and wave your hand over the tube. (You must make the magic motion that "causes" the silks to appear.)

8

Reach inside and slowly pull out the items you stuffed in the tube earlier. If you are using a streamer of silks, hand one end to someone in the front row and then slowly walk backward, allowing the streamer of silks to extend so everyone can see.

SECRET STUFF

Don't ignore step 7. It is, in many ways, the most important step. As magicians, we sometimes get caught up in how an effect works or making sure we do every step properly. But for our audiences, we're making *magic,* and that means that in every effect we have to take the time to actually do some magic. This might be as simple as waving a hand or a wand, or saying a magic word, or it might require us to close our eyes for several seconds of deep concentration. But we must always pretend to do something to make the magic happen.

COMING TO LIFE

The magician causes a partner to instantly appear onstage! This is the perfect illusion for a team or group of friends to perform. Everyone has a role to play, and each person must rely on the others to do their job. Only when everyone is working together does the illusion look perfect. (And when it does look perfect, you can win a talent show with this illusion.)

HOW IT WORKS

YOUR PARTNER IS HIDING BEHIND ONE OF THE PANELS ONSTAGE AND JUMPS INTO VIEW AT JUST THE RIGHT TIME.

What You Need

- **TWO LARGE, LIGHTWEIGHT PANELS**
  Make the panels out of stiff poster board, or ask an adult to nail together a lightweight wooden frame that you can fill in with rolled lightweight cardboard. The panels should be about 4 feet wide and 6 feet tall (these dimensions can be smaller if the performers are shorter—about 4 inches higher than the tallest performer). Place a pin or hook through the back of one panel because, during the effect, you need to quickly hang something from it. Cut out a handle for each panel and you're set.
- **FOUR PEOPLE**
  You, the magician (of course), and three partners.
- **TWO IDENTICAL COSTUMES**
  The idea in this illusion is that you display a costume and then make a person appear *wearing* the costume—in seconds. Pretty cool. For this, you need two identical costumes, one for your partner to wear and one to display on a hanger.
- **MUSIC**
  Pick something fun and upbeat. (If you go with a cowboy theme, you might want country or banjo music.)
- **A HANGER**

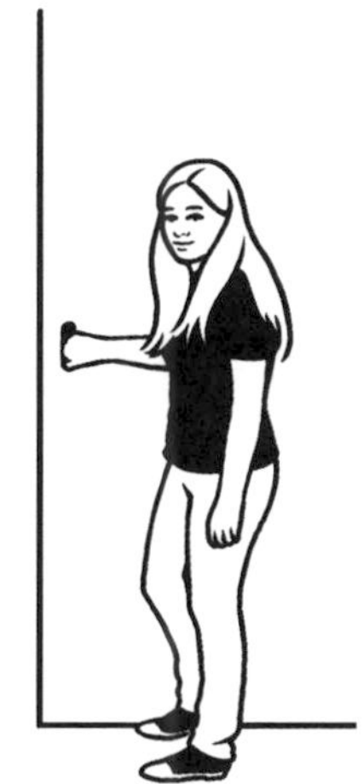

1 SETUP

This one is *all about timing*: If everyone doesn't get the timing absolutely perfect, there is no magic. So, you will want to rehearse this until it's just right. The two panels begin at the extreme sides of the stage. The "secret" partner—the one wearing the costume—begins behind the panel at stage left. The two other partners are stationed in front of each panel, ready to pull them toward the center of the stage. You, the magician, have yet to make your entrance.

2 PERFORMANCE

Start the music. Begin by walking onstage holding the hanger with the costume. Let's say it's a cowboy outfit. Display it, remove the hat for a moment, and then replace it on top of the hanger.

HIDDEN VIEW

3

When you're ready to make a partner appear, have the helpers slide the panels across the stage so that they cross each other at the very point where you are standing. Decide in advance whose panel will go in front and whose panel will go behind you.

HIDDEN VIEW

4

As the helpers slide the panels, the secret partner walks quietly and carefully *behind* the panel, hidden from view. She will not be seen as long as she stays very close to the panel and takes short, quick, quiet steps. There is strong misdirection here, because there are *two* panels and a magician, all attracting the audience's attention.

HIDDEN VIEW

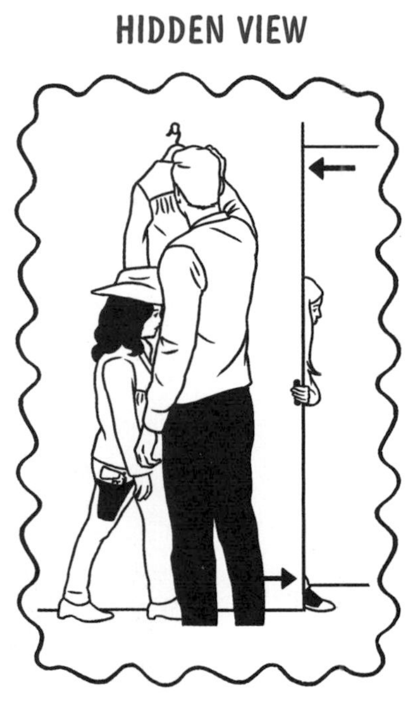

5

The moment the panels cross, two things happen: 1) You place the hanger you're holding onto the hook on the back of the panel. 2) At the same time, your costumed partner jumps into position next to you. Make sure your partner occupies the same place as the costume on the hanger just a moment ago.

6

The helpers continue to slide their panels to the opposite sides of the stage. They should never stop or even slow down as you make the exchange. It should look like the partner appears the *second* the panels cross. At performance speed, this looks really, really amazing.

SECRET STUFF

There are two areas you have to focus on: the moment the exchange is made, and making sure that your helpers keep the panels completely flat. If they lift up even a little, the audience is sure to notice the feet that aren't supposed to be there.

EGG-STRAORDINARY

You show both sides of a small screen with beautiful Chinese lettering on it. You roll the screen into a tube and drop out a real egg! Perform this up close or for a room full of people.

HOW IT WORKS

THE EGG IS BEHIND THE SCREEN THE WHOLE TIME, HANGING FROM A STRING.

What You Need

- **A SCREEN**
  Finding an authentic Chinese screen is difficult, but you can make one using a place mat that you may already have at home. The place mat should be very flexible—the kind made of very thin bamboo sticks and woven together with string. Borrow one from the dining room, but make sure you explain that it won't be coming back. (Just tell Mom and Dad that this magic effect is going to make you very, very famous. They'll understand.)
- **PAINT OR PERMANENT MARKERS (OPTIONAL)**
- **SCISSORS**
- **THREAD**
  To match the color of the egg.
- **CLEAR PACKING TAPE**
  Clear packing tape is best because it's much stronger than regular clear tape.
- **AN EGG**
- **A CLEAR DRINKING GLASS**

1 SETUP

For decorative purposes, paint Chinese lettering on both sides of the place mat. I prefer to use characters that mean "luck" and "magic." This part is optional, but the decoration helps your participants "see" a mystical screen, and not a borrowed place mat.

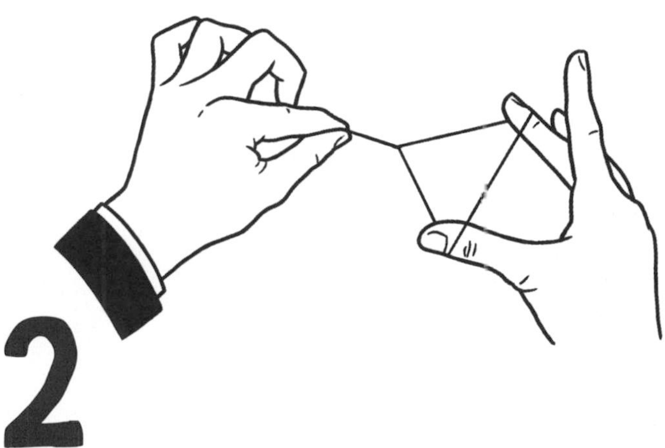

2

Next, carefully cut and tie the thread into a 5-inch loop.

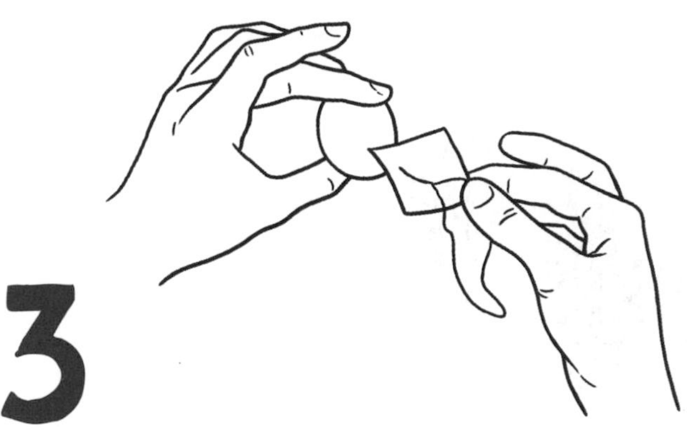

3

Tape the loop of thread to the base of the egg. Make sure it is secure.

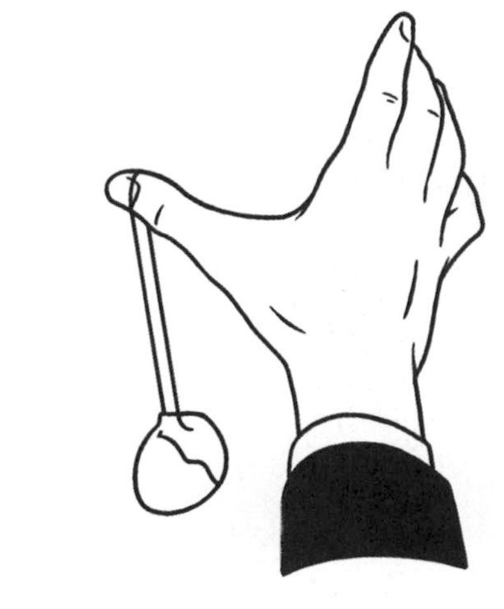

4

Place the loop of thread over your right thumb to test your contraption: The egg should dangle freely from the thread without falling.

HIDDEN VIEW

5

Just before you're ready to perform, loop the thread onto your right thumb and grasp the screen along one of the short ends between your right thumb and fingers. You can do this in your magic case or out of the audience's view.

6 PERFORMANCE

When you come into view, it should look as though you're holding a screen and nothing more.

HIDDEN VIEW

7

Next you will show that nothing is hiding behind either side of the screen with an ancient, clever maneuver: With your left thumb and fingers, pinch the lower, short end of the screen.

HIDDEN VIEW

8

Lift this end up, toward the audience, until it is even with the top end. Pinch both ends in your right hand and hold the screen in a folded position.

Using your right fingers, drop the outermost end of the screen while still holding the innermost end. This is a fancy way of showing both sides of the screen—*without* revealing the dangling egg hidden behind. Repeat this move (steps 6–9) several times. Point out the meaning of the Chinese symbols on each side of the screen as you display them.

To produce the egg, grasp the bottom end of the screen and fold it *inside* so that it is even with the upper end. Carefully release the egg from your thumb so it is concealed inside the screen.

Say, *"This magic screen can produce anything we want. Help me say the magic words: cock-a-doodle-doo!"* Gently roll the screen around the egg to form a narrow tube, and ask the audience to shout "cocka-doodle-doo" with you.

Wave your hands over the tube, and then snap your fingers, carefully allowing the egg to roll from the tube into your hand. When you catch the egg, hold it so that the thread is covered by your fingers. From a few feet away, the thread will not be noticed.

13

To prove the egg is real, put the tube down, pick up the glass, and crack the egg into it. Toss the shells (along with the secret loop of thread) into the glass, too, where no one is likely to see the thread.

SECRET STUFF

Producing an egg is a pretty amazing feat because audiences know how fragile eggs are, and how impossible it would be to hide or manipulate something that could break so easily. But if you're performing over a carpet or you don't want to use an egg, you can use lots of other cool objects—a large piece of candy or a small stuffed animal both work well.

TRICKY TABLE

So, you've mastered your favorite effects from this book, and now you're booked to perform at your neighbor's barbecue. The question is, what will you perform on? If you're serious about performing, you're going to need a performer's table.

My first magic table wasn't really a table at all—it was my dad's old television stand! I chose to use it because it was on wheels. The wheels came in handy when I was rolling it onstage and off. For that reason, printer stands and microwave carts also work great. Just cover the outside with colorful fabric, and use Velcro to attach a sign to the front. Set your props on the shelves below until you're ready to perform with them. You should also keep a big plastic tub or trunk nearby. This is where you carry your props between shows. Everything should have its place, so as you finish each effect, you can dump it in the tub and go on to your next miracle.

PANDORA'S BOX

In this stunning show of conjuring, the magician makes his partner appear from an empty box. "Pandora's Box" requires nothing more than a partner, a large box, and a little rehearsal.

HOW IT WORKS

YOUR PARTNER CRAWLS OUT OF AND THEN BACK INTO THE BOX, TIMING IT SO THE AUDIENCE DOESN'T SEE BEFORE HE OR SHE APPEARS.

What You Need

- A LARGE BOX (PLUS A CRAFT KNIFE OR SCISSORS, DUCT TAPE, MARKERS, AND A RULER) Your partner must be able to both fit in and secretly crawl in and out of the box, so use either a small partner (like a little brother or sister) or a big box.
- A PARTNER
- LIVELY MUSIC

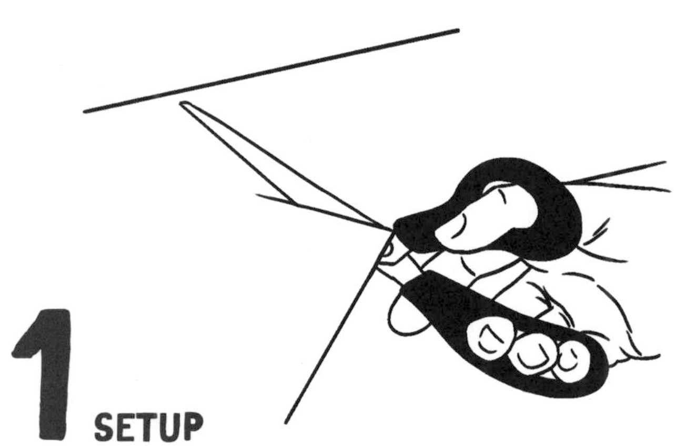

1 SETUP

Ask an adult to help prepare the box. Cut off the flaps and place the box upside down on your performance surface (the bottom is open).

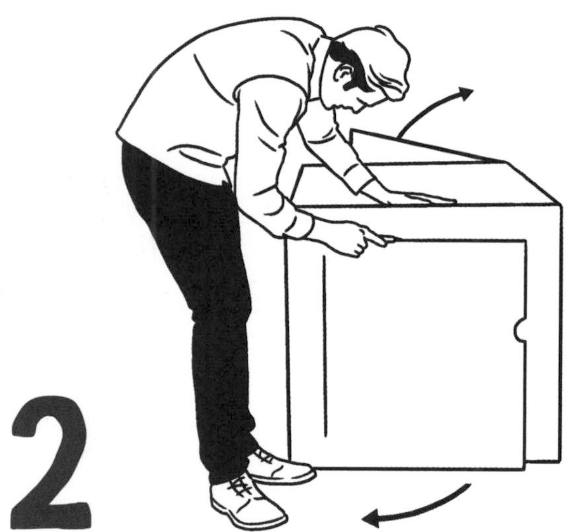

2

Cut two doors on opposite sides of the box, one that opens to the left and one that opens to the right. Make sure the doors are as large as possible and reach the floor. The doors should take up almost the complete side of the box.

3

It's important that when you open the doors, they stay open. Some cardboard is very stiff, causing the doors to spring back to a closed position. (If this is the case, cut off the doors completely and then reattach them, hinging them with duct tape.) We'll call the door that is downstage, nearest the audience, the "front door." The upstage door, away from the audience, will be called the "back door."

4

If you want to decorate the box, use markers to make it look like a tiny house with doors and a roof, or simply present the illusion as if it's an ordinary box (and actually, it is!).

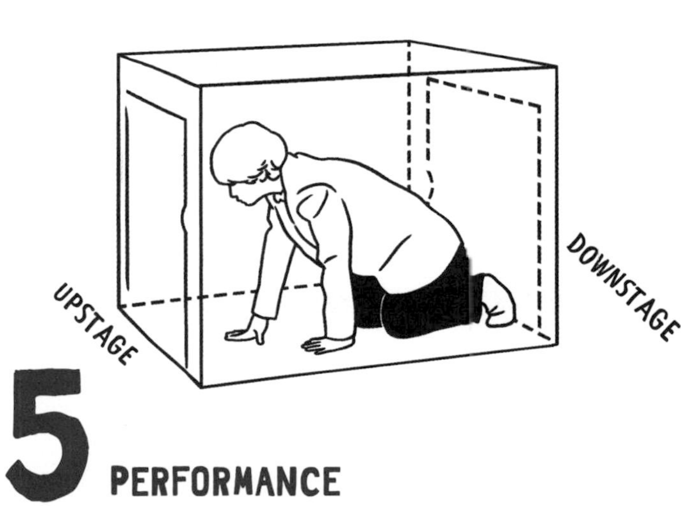

5 PERFORMANCE

The box begins in the middle of the stage with your partner hidden inside (underneath). He should face the upstage door, ready to secretly crawl out in a moment.

6

You, the magician, walk out to music and approach the box. Without lifting it, rotate the box all the way around to show off any decorations, as well as the doors in front and behind. Your partner remains perfectly still.

7

Open the back door first and make sure it stays open. The back of the door will be visible from the audience to the right of the box. It will act as a secret shield.

HIDDEN VIEW

8

Now your partner secretly crawls out of the box and hides behind the back door.

9

While your partner is crawling, you walk slowly around the box and, once your partner is hidden, open the front door.

10

With both doors open, your partner is hiding behind the back door and the audience can now see all the way through the empty box. Nobody's home (. . . yet!).

> **SECRET STUFF**
>
> There are endless themes for this illusion. Decorate the box like a doghouse and introduce the effect by explaining that you're upset because your dog went missing. When your partner appears, he could be holding a stuffed animal dog, or dressed in a dog costume, or even holding a real (quiet) dog. If you decorate the box like a dollhouse, you can make a real "live" doll appear!

11

Close the front door, and slowly walk around the box to the back.

HIDDEN VIEW

12

As soon as the front door is closed, your partner secretly crawls back into the box, and you continue to walk around the box to close the back door.

13

Now, after all that buildup, clap your hands together and lift the box upward quickly. As you do, your partner immediately stands. (When you time it right, it looks as though he appears just *as* you whisk the box away.) It's as if he materializes in a standing position.

THUMBTHING COOL

If your family is anything like mine, you have an uncle who has one or two tricks in his repertoire: He pretends to "steal your nose" by placing his thumb between his fingers and pretending to pull your nose from your face, *or* he pretends to remove his thumb. Pretty basic stuff. *This* is the ultimate version of finger magic—you stretch your thumb to three times its normal length!

YOUR *OTHER* THUMB IS A DECOY. WHEN YOU LINE UP YOUR THUMBS IN JUST THE RIGHT WAY, IT LOOKS LIKE YOU HAVE ONE VERY, VERY LONG THUMB.

What You Need

☞ YOUR TWO THUMBS!

1 **PERFORMANCE**

Your starting position is to gently bite the tip of your left thumb between your teeth.

2

Make your left fingers into a fist and press the pad of your thumb against your curled left first finger.

3

When you're ready to make your thumb grow, wrap your right fingers around your left fist. Place your right thumb on top of and behind your left thumb.

4

Breathe in and lean back slightly, and as you exhale and lean forward, you do the secret move . . .

5

Slide your *right* thumb between your teeth as you slide your left thumb into your loosely cupped right fingers. Keep your right thumb pad near your right first finger, so that the way you hold your right hand matches the way you were just holding your left.

Continue by sliding your left fist below your right, so they are stacked on top of each other.

Separate your fists just a little but keep your left thumb connected to your right fist.

8

In a continuous motion, move both fists downward, allowing your right thumb to extend fully from the right fist. When completely extended, it looks like you're holding one very, very long thumb. Hold this position for only a second.

To finish the illusion, bring both hands back together as if you're pushing your thumb back against your teeth. As the fists come together, switch thumbs again, so the left thumb is pinched between your teeth, and drop your right hand to your side.

To finish, give a couple of small tugs on your left thumb again, as if it's still stretchable.

BREAKAWAY BOX

This is a magic box that causes objects (a phone, a hat, your homework!) to disappear or change into other objects. You can use this box as a stand-alone effect, or incorporate it into other effects (like Hat Trick, page 53) you'll explore later on. It's definitely worth building now, because it's going to be one of your go-to illusions.

HOW IT WORKS

THERE IS A TOP-SECRET COMPARTMENT INSIDE THE BOX THAT YOU CAN HIDE THINGS IN.

What You Need

- ☞ TWO LARGE CEREAL BOXES
  You can redecorate the boxes by painting over the panels or, if you can find the Trix brand of cereal (there is a rabbit waving a magic wand on the box, so you don't have to redecorate), get two of those.
- ☞ SCISSORS
- ☞ CLEAR TAPE
- ☞ CONFETTI (OPTIONAL)

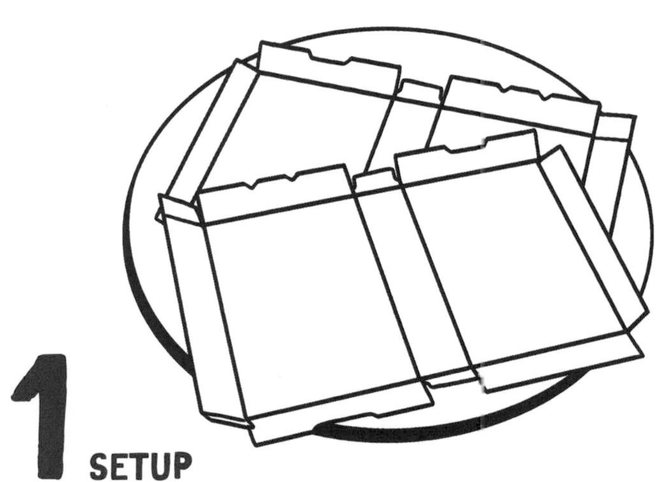

1 SETUP

To make the secret compartment in one of the cereal boxes, carefully pry open all the panels of both boxes so that they can lie flat on your work surface.

2

Choose one box to use in the performance, and set it aside. Cut one large panel from the other cereal box, leaving one large panel with the sides still attached. Trim the sides into triangles and trim away the bottom tab entirely, as shown.

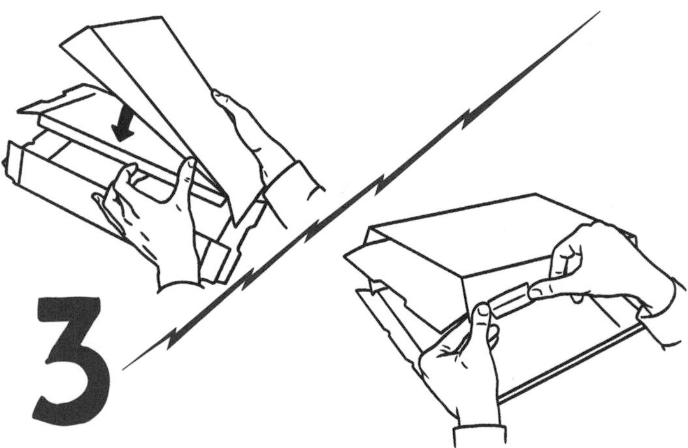

3

Tape the cutout panel to the outside back panel of the second box, creating a new compartment big enough to hold whatever you want to vanish. If it's something small, like a cell phone, you can make the compartment quite small (½ inch deep). If it's something bigger, like a hat, make the compartment 1 to 2 inches deep.

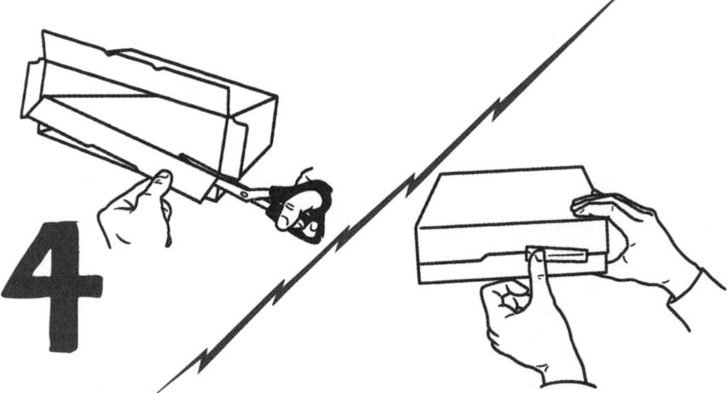

4

Re-form the box shape so the compartment appears *inside* the box. (*Note:* You may have to cut off any tabs from the original box that are sticking up that might give away the secret compartment.) Apply a small piece of clear tape in one upper corner so that the box will stay formed until you give it a firm flick. (You'll replace this tape each time you perform.) You can fill the box with handfuls of confetti to make the vanish look super-cool.

5 PERFORMANCE

When you are ready to perform, display any object you wish to make disappear in your right hand, and hold the box in your left. Shoes, hats, or small toys work well. Let's assume you want to make a mobile phone disappear.

6

Pretend to place the phone inside the box, but actually slide it securely inside the secret compartment.

7

When you are ready to make the phone vanish, flick the box open with your fingers, so the front panel falls open and flat, and the confetti falls to the floor. *Whoosh*. The phone is gone!

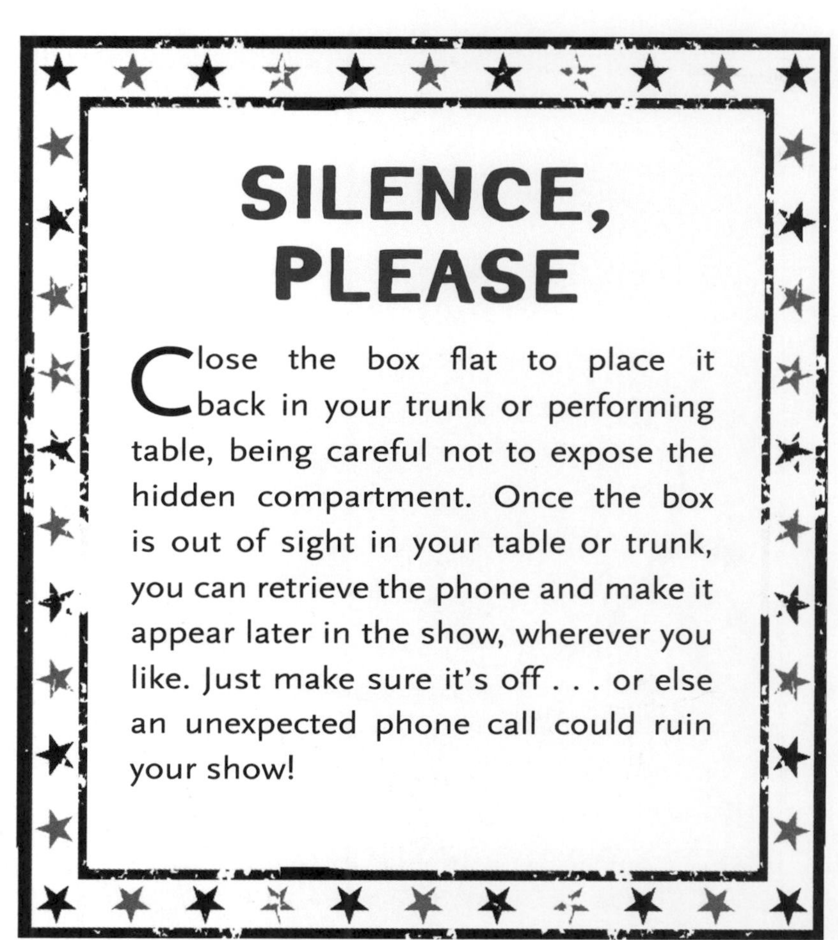

SILENCE, PLEASE

Close the box flat to place it back in your trunk or performing table, being careful not to expose the hidden compartment. Once the box is out of sight in your table or trunk, you can retrieve the phone and make it appear later in the show, wherever you like. Just make sure it's off . . . or else an unexpected phone call could ruin your show!

HAT TRICK

You make a baseball cap appear on a volunteer's head! This is a unique effect because the audience will "see" how you make a hat appear on the participant's head, but your volunteer will have absolutely no idea. The fun comes from her reaction, when she realizes that you made a hat appear on her head without her feeling it. It's fun for everyone, but for different reasons.

HOW IT WORKS

YOU USE THE BREAKAWAY BOX (PAGE 50) TO MAKE THE HAT DISAPPEAR. TO CAUSE THE HAT TO REAPPEAR ON A PARTICIPANT'S HEAD, YOU USE A DUPLICATE HAT.

What You Need

- ☞ TWO IDENTICAL BASEBALL CAPS
  You can use any kind of hat, really, or even make paper hats, as long as the brim is stiff enough to stay open on its own (cold weather ski hats won't work).
- ☞ BREAKAWAY BOX
  Use the one you made for "Breakaway Box," page 50.
- ☞ CLEAR TAPE
- ☞ CONFETTI

1 SETUP

Place one cap in view, perhaps on a table, and hide the other one with your props or in your back pocket. Have the Breakaway Box set up (taped shut) on your table, with a few fistfuls of confetti inside.

2 PERFORMANCE

Invite a volunteer onstage and ask her to face forward. Make *sure* she faces forward throughout the effect, or else this isn't going to work. Retrieve the cap from your table and display it to everyone, including your volunteer.

3

Then, place the cap *backward* on her head, so the brim is out of her sight. This illusion works best if the cap is loose fitting. Say, *"In a moment, I will cause this cap to disappear and reappear in the most unexpected way. This is an illusion just for (insert the name of your volunteer), so please don't spoil it for her, audience!"* Wink at the audience, and warn them not to shout anything.

4

Stand behind your volunteer and secretly retrieve the duplicate hat. Grasp the hat from above and place it over the original hat on the volunteer's head. Press firmly for a moment and pull away, taking the duplicate hat and leaving the original hat on the volunteer.

5

Immediately hand the duplicate cap to your volunteer and ask her to hold it with both hands, outstretched. With both hands occupied, she will be unable to feel the top of her head and won't realize she is still wearing a cap. A lot is going on here: The volunteer will "feel" you remove her cap, even though you faked it. As crazy as it might sound, she will be unable to feel the cap on her head, and she will think that what she felt was you removing her cap and handing it to her.

6

The audience sees it differently. They see both caps, and of course they realize your volunteer is still wearing her cap. But they *also* will see that she has absolutely no idea she is still wearing it! This will cause some participants to giggle, so you may have to remind them not to give anything away.

NEURAL ADAPTATION

Many magic effects are really just science in disguise. Hat Trick works because of a principle that scientists call "neural adaptation." This is the idea that your brain "senses" something that you feel for only a few seconds. Then, your body adapts to whatever you are touching or feeling, and you stop feeling it. For example, if you place your hand on a table, you can feel the table's cold surface against your palm. But if you hold still, after a few seconds, you really can't feel the table anymore. Your eyes can see that the table is there pressed against your hand, but the table becomes your new "normal," and you don't actively feel the pressure between the surfaces.

In Hat Trick, the volunteer feels you place the cap on her head. But then, after a few moments, the neural adaptation sets in, and the feeling of the cap becomes her new normal, and she won't actively feel it on her head. It's just there. So when you remove one cap, and fool her eyes by showing her what looks like the cap you just removed, she will have no idea she is still wearing a baseball cap.

7

Take back the duplicate cap and place it in the secret compartment of the Breakaway Box. (Make sure your volunteer is still watching.) Wave your hands over the box and then open it forward, showing that the box is empty. The confetti falls out, and the hat has disappeared!

8

To your volunteer, you say, *"And now, I will make the hat appear in the most unexpected place . . . back on your head!"* Allow her to reach up and discover that she is *wearing* the cap she just saw you place inside the box. You made it reappear on her head without her feeling it. The audience will be amazed that the cap disappeared, and although they will know how you made it appear on your volunteer's head, her reaction makes the whole effect fun.

SECRET STUFF

Effects like this are all about the volunteer's reaction, so it's important to choose someone who is fun, who will listen to your instructions, and who has the confidence to act naturally onstage, in front of lots of people. In other words, choose someone who *wants* to come up. The best way to do this is to say, *"I need a volunteer for my next effect. Raise your hand if you want to help."* Only kids who want to come up will raise their hands. And note that the kids who remain seated, raising their hands politely, will probably follow directions better than the kids jumping out of their seats and yelling at you.

ORNA-MENTAL

To bring a little magic to your family's holiday party, you offer to perform a Christmas miracle: Ask your family to choose a participant to pick an ornament off the tree while you step out of the room. When you return, point to the chosen ornament and reveal the person who thought of it!

One of the greatest qualities about magic is that it brings people closer together and gives everyone a fun memory. When you're with your family for the holidays, you have the opportunity to create a legendary moment that will be talked about among your family for many years to come.

HOW IT WORKS

YOU USE A SECRET CODE AND A SECRET PARTNER, WHO TELLS YOU WHICH ORNAMENT WAS CHOSEN WITHOUT EVEN SAYING A WORD.

What You Need

☞ A SECRET PARTNER
You need to choose a partner to work secretly with you. It should be someone trustworthy, because even though it's your effect, *the partner* does most of the work. Parents are great for this.

☞ A CHRISTMAS TREE WITH ORNAMENTS
The cool thing is, it can be *any* Christmas tree, as long as it has lots of different ornaments on it. Some people are very particular about their Christmas trees. Because you will be telling the audience to move ornaments from branch to branch, always ask first if you can invite people to touch the tree. Usually families don't mind, but you should always ask first.

1 SETUP

With your partner, secretly agree on two codes: a "key" ornament, which can be anywhere on the tree (maybe it's the Santa Teddy Bear ornament) and the second code, which will involve mimicking someone else in the room.

> SECRET STUFF
>
> I started magic when I was seven, and since that time, my family always asks me to do magic at our holiday party. I always wanted to come up with something using a Christmas tree, and so I invented "Orna-Mental."

2 PERFORMANCE

You say, *"I would like to show everyone a mystery. On most occasions I would say, 'Pick a card, any card.' But because it's Christmas and I have no deck, I thought we could use this tree. I will ask someone to pick an ornament, any ornament! The way it works is this: I will leave the room. When I do, I would like everyone to choose my participant. It can be anyone at all. I would like that person to walk over to the tree and pick any ornament off the tree, show it around, and place it on a different branch. Everyone help remember the chosen ornament."*

3

You continue, *"Then, you have to shuffle the tree! Everyone can move ornaments around from branch to branch. And when you're done, send someone to get me. When I come back, don't say a word about which ornament was chosen or who chose it."* You leave the room and wait for your family and friends to complete the instructions you have given them, and then come get you.

4

When you walk back into the room, examine the tree carefully, looking at it up and down, and then pick out the chosen ornament . . . to huge applause! What has actually happened is that your secret partner has *told* you which ornament was chosen, using the predetermined code.

5

Your partner (who was helping "shuffle" the tree with the rest of the family) will have placed the key ornament *right next to* the chosen ornament. So when you look at the tree, just look for the Santa Teddy, and you know the ornament right next to it will be the chosen ornament. Here, the chosen ornament is a star.

6

Your partner has also studied precisely how the participant is standing and stands in the exact same way. For example, if your participant has both hands in her pockets and she is swaying from side to side, your secret partner will put both hands in his pockets and sway, too. If your participant scratches her back for a moment, your secret partner will scratch *his* back a few seconds later. Just stare at everyone carefully, as if you can't decide who the participant was. In the example shown, the secret partner is on the right side with his hand on his hip. Once you see how he is standing, you can easily tell who is standing in the same way. In this case, it's the woman wearing boots.

7

Once you've determined who the participant is, look over the crowd once more and announce, *"Not only that, but I believe Aunt Pam was the one who chose the ornament!"* Your family will be amazed.

DUCKS AND MAGICIANS

If you observe a duck in the water, he looks graceful and relaxed. But under the water, he's paddling as fast as he can. Magicians are like ducks. If you watch a show, everything looks smooth. But as you have learned, magicians are doing a lot of secret stuff.

It is the magician's job to make difficult feats look easy, but in Orna-Mental you must really ham it up to make this easy effect *look* difficult. Don't just walk into the living room and point out the chosen ornament. Instead, look the tree up and down, and give some commentary: *"Hmm. If Grandpa was the participant, I could see him taking the blue ornament because that's his favorite color. This is the prettiest ornament, so maybe it was chosen. But then again, nobody would choose something so obvious."* Really make them think you're guessing, and that maybe you made a lucky guess. Then, when you turn around and reveal who the participant was, it will seem even more impressive.

5

Now go back through and create color drawings on all the even pages. If you want to be very detailed, try to duplicate the drawings you made on the other pages, but color them in. (If you drew a giraffe on the first page of your notebook, for example, make a *color* drawing of a giraffe on the second page. If you drew your house on the fifth page, make a color drawing of your house on the sixth page.) Take your time and color inside the lines.

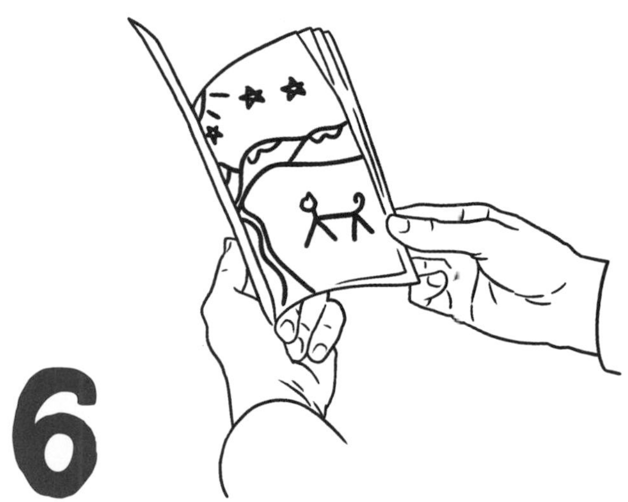

6

To test that your amazing notebook works, flip through the booklet by letting the pages flick off your thumb near the lower right corner. You should see *only* black-and-white drawings from cover to cover.

7

Now flip through again, this time flicking the pages from the upper right corner. It should look like color magically filled the very same pages!

8

Practice displaying the notebook at chest height with the pages facing the audience. The best way to practice this is in front of a mirror. Hold the booklet at the top (or bottom) corner, and let the pages flip off your thumb and fingers page by page.

9 PERFORMANCE

To perform, present your magic notebook to the audience.

10

Flip through it from the lower right corner. Say, *"I love to draw, and this is where I put all my best ideas. These are drawings of the things I like, or the things I'm thinking about. The problem is, I haven't had time to color them in. Would you help me?"*

11

Continue, *"I want you to reach into the air and grab some imaginary color, like this."* Reach into the air with one hand and make a fist. *"This is a handful of red."*

12

Point at someone in the first row and say, *"Oh nice! We needed some green."* Then to someone else: *"And I see you have some yellow in your hand. Perfect."* Invite everyone to throw his or her imaginary color into your notebook.

13

Dramatically flip through the notebook again, this time from the upper right corner. All the pages have been filled in with color!

SECRET STUFF

Flip through the pages slowly. Even professional magicians often flip through too fast. You can stop briefly on every page that flicks off your finger to give the audience a good look at your drawing. Then, at the end, when they see the same drawings colored in, they will be able to identify the same themes you showed them in black and white—making the illusion all the more effective.

BRANCHING OUT

You display several pages from a small newspaper and roll them into a tube. Within seconds, you manage to grow a paper tree that is taller than you are!

HOW IT WORKS

THE "NEWSPAPER TREE" IS AN OLD STUNT THAT ALLOWS YOU TO TEAR AND UNFOLD A NEWSPAPER INTO A VERY LONG TUBE. BY SECRETLY PREPARING THE NEWSPAPER IN ADVANCE, IT WILL APPEAR THAT YOU CAN PERFORM THIS STUNT IMPROMPTU.

What You Need

- NEWSPAPER
  You need only single sheets, not the kind with a fold in the middle. And the smaller the newspaper size, the better, though you can always trim the newspaper to size if need be.
- TWO RUBBER BANDS
- SCISSORS
- TAPE

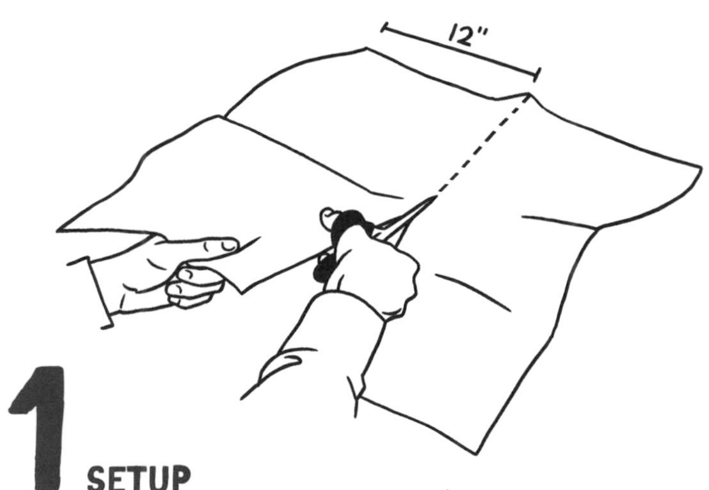

1 SETUP

First, prepare the newspaper for the tree (you'll attach this part to a newspaper that you can display to the audience). Begin by setting eight sheets of newspaper on the table. This will work best if the newspaper is only about 12 inches wide, cut it to the proper size.

2

Roll the stack of newspaper sheets into a tube.

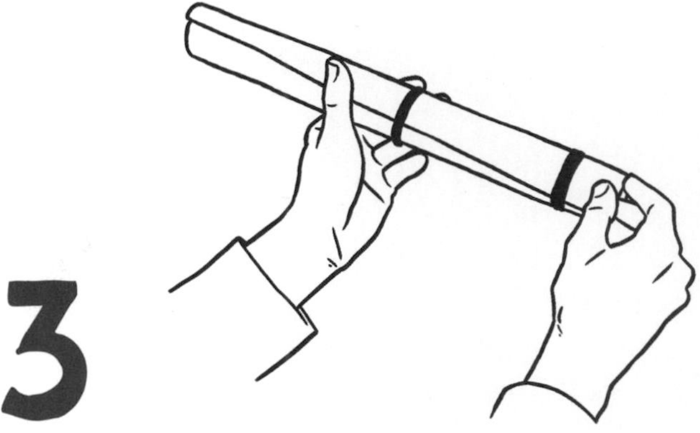

3

Keeping the paper tightly rolled, place a rubber band near the bottom and the center of the tube.

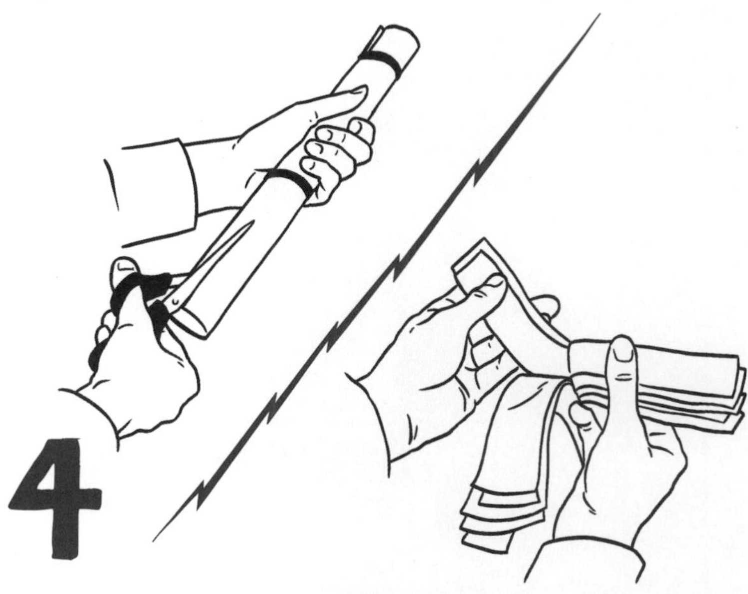

4

With scissors, carefully cut three evenly spaced slits from the top of the newspaper roll about halfway down the tube. Now the tube is ready. (When you peel back the three sections you just cut—don't do this just yet—you will create the "leaves" for the tree. When you pull the center out, you will see the tree grow right before your eyes!)

5

Center the tube horizontally, on an uncut sheet of newspaper. You don't have to tape it neatly because nobody will ever see this part. Just make sure you only tape between the rubber bands (leave the cut section alone), and make sure it's secure. Place a couple of additional pages of newspaper in front of the prepared piece and you're ready to perform.

HIDDEN VIEW

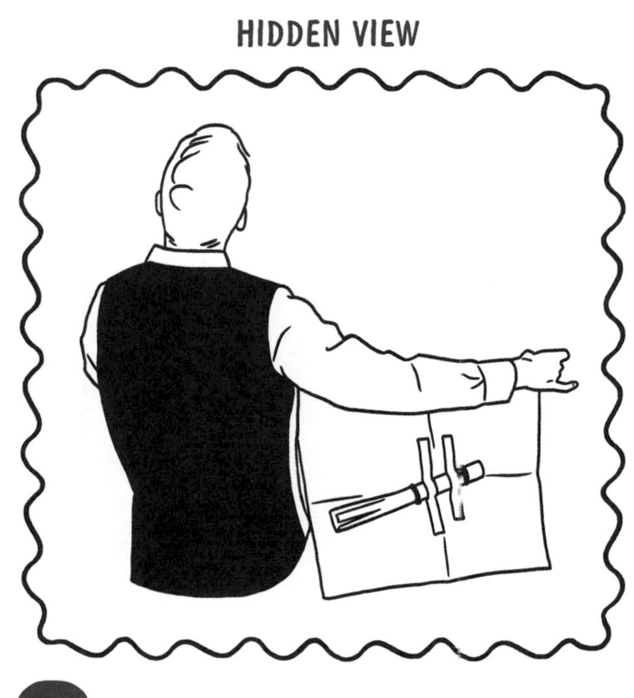

6 PERFORMANCE

Present the stack of newspaper pages in your left hand, making sure you don't show the back of the stack (where the tube is hidden).

7

Show the pages individually, front and back, but don't show the back of the prepared page.

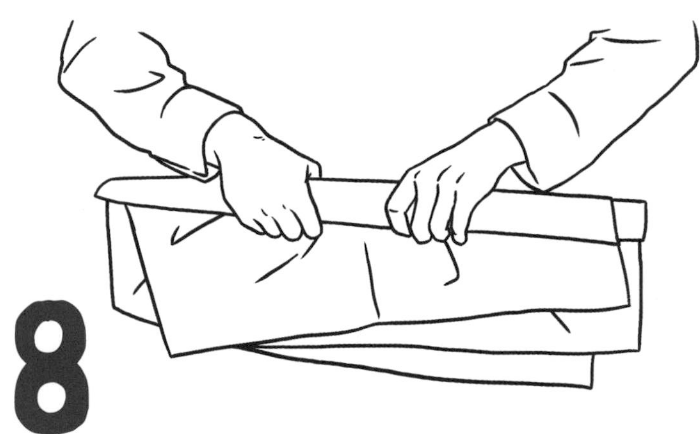

8

Restack the pages and then roll them into a tight tube.

SECRET STUFF

Experiment with how tightly you wrap the newspaper with rubber bands. If you wrap them very tightly, the tree is harder to unfold but sturdier. If you wrap them very loosely, the tree will be quite flimsy, but you can simply hold the middle of the tube over your hand and allow the bottom of the tree to drop to the floor, creating the tree sculpture as it drops.

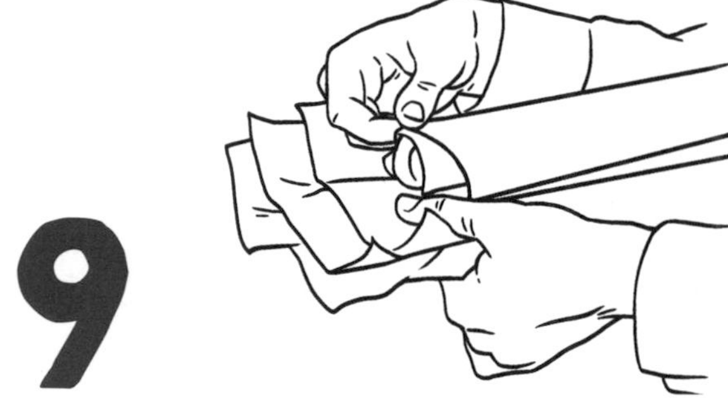

9

Say, *"Newspapers are made of paper, and paper is made from trees. I would like to change this newspaper back into a tree."* That's really all you need to say. As you talk, tear away the unprepared newspaper at the end of the tube nearest the cut side of the prepared tube. This way you can more easily reach the paper tree you've already prepared.

10

One by one, peel down the three sections of the paper tree you prepared. As you do, comment that, *"All trees start small, like the one I'm holding."*

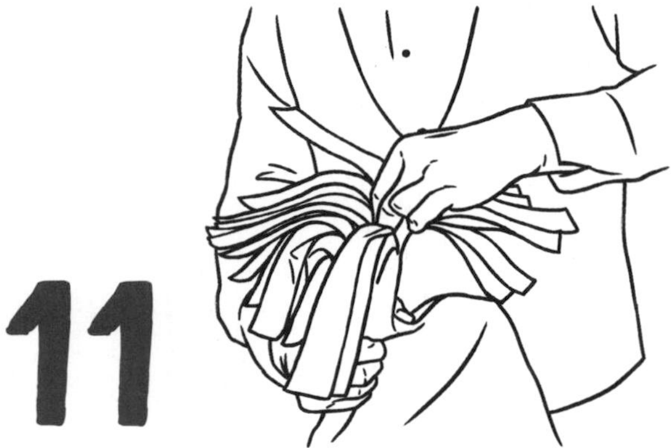

11

Wedge two fingers into the middle of the paper tree and brace the newspaper with your other hand.

12

Separate your hands widely, extending the pages of the newspaper and twisting as your hands move apart. Don't pull the pieces too hard or you risk pulling them entirely from the tube.

13

When you're done, you should be left holding a very sturdy newspaper tree.

TRAVELING JUICE

You present an empty top hat, a cup of juice, and an empty paper bag. What happens next is unbelievable: You cause the juice to travel invisibly from the paper bag into the top hat!

HOW IT WORKS
YOU USE AN EXTRA CUP THE AUDIENCE ISN'T AWARE OF.

What You Need

☞ TWO PAPER CUPS
Use two paper cups that you can stack together, one inside the other. With a casual glance, these cups don't *look* like two cups—the two should just blend together and look like one. Don't use clear plastic or Styrofoam cups.

☞ A SMALL PAPER BAG

☞ A TOP HAT
A top hat works great, but you could also decorate an empty tissue box and use that, or use your dad's cowboy hat. (Note: This only works if your dad is a cowboy.)

☞ A BOTTLE OF JUICE
Alternatively, you can use a can of soda (I wasn't allowed to drink it when I was a kid, so I went with juice).

1 SETUP

Place the cups, paper bag, hat, and juice on the table.

2 PERFORMANCE

Display the hat and have it examined. Do the same with the paper bag. Now present the stacked cups as one cup. If you treat them like one cup and make sure they don't come apart, everyone will think you have just one.

3

Lower the cup inside the top hat (slightly to one side) and say, *"Magicians wear hats like this one because hats help with the magic. In a moment I will make this cup appear in this hat, like this. But to make it more difficult, I will fill the cup with juice."*

4

Reach into the hat and, with one hand, carefully slide one cup from the other. Lift the inner cup and display it for a moment.

HIDDEN VIEW

5

Replace the cup you're holding back in the hat *next to the other cup*. The participants can't see inside the hat, so they can't see that you now have two cups side by side.

HIDDEN VIEW

6

Pour the juice from the bottle into one of the cups. Be careful here, or you could later be wearing a wet hat. Open the paper bag and place it on a table at the other side of the stage.

7

Now pick up the empty cup from the hat, holding it as if it were full of juice.

8

You can even pretend to take a sip.

9

Place the empty cup into the bag. Do this carefully, slowly, and with a delicate touch. Just pretend it really is full of juice.

10

Wave your hand over the bag, still holding it very gently. Announce that you will make the juice and the cup disappear.

19: TRAVELING JUICE

11

Now smack your hands together quickly, crushing the bag and the paper cup. *Thwack!*

12

Roll the bag into a tight ball and toss it over your shoulder. The cup of juice disappeared!

13

"That juice didn't go too far," you say with a smile. Walk over to the top hat, reach inside, and retrieve the full cup of juice.

14

Toast your audience . . .

15

. . . and take a well-deserved sip of juice.

SECRET STUFF

The best magicians adapt to their environment. You won't always have time to prepare effects like this one, but that's okay. You just *adapt*, because you can perform this almost anywhere, impromptu. For example, suppose you want to perform Traveling Juice at a picnic. Most picnics have paper cups, so you're good there. You could use a picnic basket instead of a top hat, and a plastic grocery bag will work instead of a paper bag.

Adelaide Herrmann: MAGIC SUPERSTAR

THROUGHOUT HISTORY, there have been many *fantastic* female magicians, but Adelaide Herrmann is my favorite. Adelaide began her career as a dancer, and then married world-famous magician Alexander Herrmann. She toured with her husband, "The Great Herrmann," to all the most famous theaters in Europe and the United States. When Alexander died in 1896, she toured with his nephew, Leon Herrmann. Then she did something quite unexpected for a woman in that period: *She* became the star magician.

Adelaide learned many difficult effects that her husband had performed, and she even added new and original illusions to the act. She was the first true female superstar in magic, and she remains a role model for many of today's great female magicians.

SPONGE SWINDLE

You show two pieces of sponge and give one to a participant. You cause one to disappear from your pocket and reappear, alongside the other one, in the participant's hand!

HOW IT WORKS

YOU USE AN EXTRA, THIRD PIECE OF SPONGE. BECAUSE THE SPONGES CAN BE SQUISHED TOGETHER QUITE SMALL, THE PARTICIPANT CAN'T FEEL WHETHER HE IS HOLDING ONE OR TWO SPONGES.

What You Need

- ☞ PANTS WITH FRONT POCKETS
- ☞ A WHITE PAPER TOWEL
- ☞ SCISSORS
- ☞ THREE PIECES OF SPONGE
  Foam sponges (the kind they pad boxes with before shipping) work best. (In a pinch, you can just wad up three pieces of paper towel.) The size of the sponges depends on the size of your hands, but aim for each one to be about the size of a clown's nose.

1 SETUP

The first step is to turn your right pocket inside out, like you're showing someone it's empty. Make sure the fabric on the inside of your pocket is white. It usually is. Now put all four corners of the paper towel together and slip the towel into your pocket, corners first. If you reach into your pocket and pull on the center of the paper towel, it should look just about like you turned your pocket inside out.

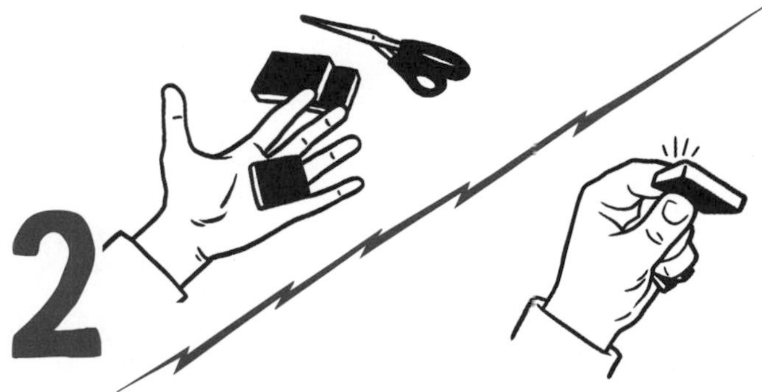

2

Hide one piece of sponge in your left hand by squishing it in your left fist. Now extend your left thumb and first finger and pinch the second sponge between your thumb and finger. It looks like you're displaying one sponge in your hand. Nobody will suspect there is another one hidden in your fist.

3

You have to make the position of both hands match each other. So, make a fist with your right hand and pinch the third sponge between your right thumb and first finger. Now you're ready to perform.

SECRET STUFF

If you want to get into this effect when people are watching, just keep the sponges in your pocket. When you place your hand in your pocket just before performing, squeeze one sponge into your fist and remove the other two with your left first finger and thumb. Transfer one sponge to your right hand and you're ready to make magic.

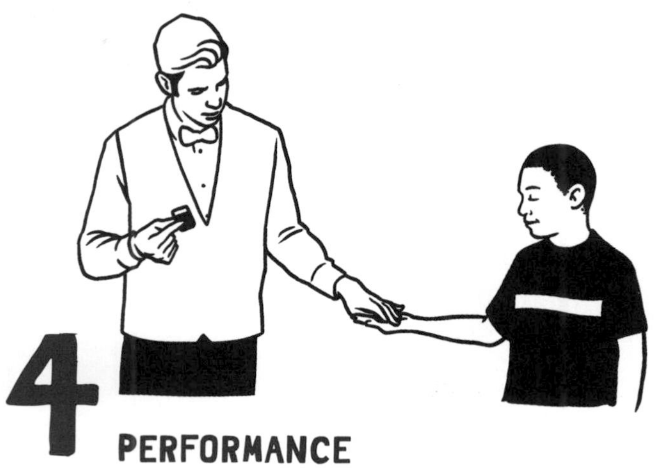

4

PERFORMANCE

Say, *"I have two pieces of sponge here. After dinner my brother and I have to wipe off the counters with these sponges. Sometimes I do magic so that he has to do twice the work. Want to see?"* Everyone will want to see this. Explain that the two sponges in your hands are for you and your brother. Ask a participant to extend his hand flat, palm up, and say, *"Would you hold on to my brother's sponge?"* With your left thumb and first finger, pull the sponge on display into your left fist and squeeze both sponges together. (It doesn't matter whether people see into your fist at this point. If they see the sponge, it will just look like the one you showed.) Pinching both sponges tightly together, place the two sponges, as one, onto your participant's hand. Have him close his hand tightly.

5

Say, *"Now all I have to do is make my sponge disappear."* Place the sponge in your right hand into your right pocket and shove it all the way to the bottom, past the paper towel. Remove your hand and show it empty as you say, *"I will make it disappear from my pocket, like this!"*

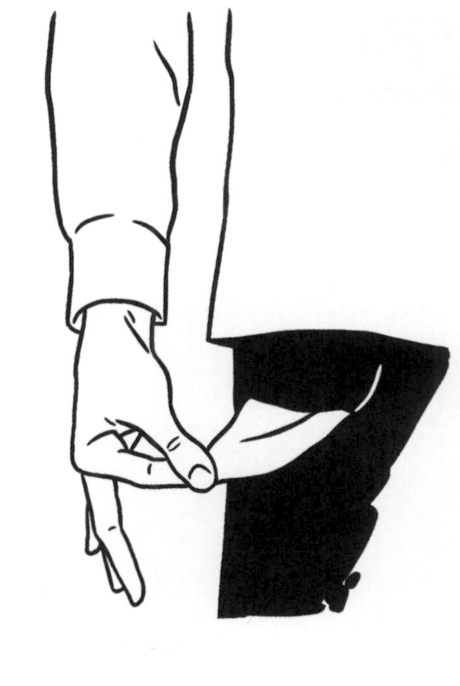

6

Reach back into your pocket and pull the paper towel out about halfway, to show that your pocket is empty.

7

Continue, *"And then all I have to do is make the sponge appear in my brother's hand . . . or in yours!"* Ask the participant to open his hand, where he will discover two sponges.

Size Isn't EVERYTHING

"KIDS CAN'T DO MAGIC," my friends would say. "They aren't big enough. Their hands are too small." As you read this book, maybe even you have doubts about your size. Well, let me tell you about Matthew Buchinger. If you think doing magic with small hands is tough, think about doing magic with *no hands at all*.

Matthew Buchinger was born in Germany in 1674, and he was born without arms or legs. Instead, he had just small stumps for arms. Despite this, Matthew Buchinger was able to perform the famous "Cups and Balls" effect, one of the most challenging feats in magic. He performed effects with cards for some of the most important people of his time.

Amazingly, he wasn't just a magician. He also played six instruments, wrote poetry, built model ships in bottles, and was an exceptional artist who could draw lines of poetry into the hair of his portraits.

Matthew Buchinger is proof that anyone who works hard can become a great magician, regardless of his or her size.

IMPROMPTU!

HANDY CANDY

You are able to find where someone hides a small piece of candy, even when you're blindfolded! This is the perfect stunt to perform at a friend's house, or when you want to amaze your parents' guests. It's also one of the rare effects that can be repeated!

HOW IT WORKS

YOU SECRETLY KNOW HOW EACH MUG IS PLACED ON THE TABLE. WHEN THE PARTICIPANT PLACES THE OBJECT UNDER ONE OF THE MUGS, YOU WILL KNOW WHICH ONE SHE LIFTED BECAUSE IT WILL BE REPLACED ON THE TABLE *SLIGHTLY* DIFFERENTLY FROM THE WAY YOU PLACED IT.

What You Need

- **THREE OR MORE MUGS**
  Use whatever you can find. If you can't find three mugs, use a mug, a cup (one you can't see through), and a bowl.
- **CANDY**
  You just need any small object, so if candy isn't available, borrow a stick of gum, a coin, or another item.
- **BLINDFOLD (OPTIONAL)**
  This is completely optional, but it works best to wear a blindfold in a formal show. If you're performing this impromptu, just have someone cover your eyes or leave the room while they're hiding the candy.
- **MARKER**

1 SETUP

Set the mugs upside down on a table. Spread them out as much as possible, so that there is a lot of empty space between each one. (You can also, for example, place three mugs on the kitchen table, one near the sink, and one on the TV stand.) Note: If you perform this onstage, place a mug on three different small tables, one at stage left, one at center stage, and one at stage right. It's best to space the mugs out because you don't want your participant to touch or move more than one mug.

2 PERFORMANCE

When you perform, you must be able to recognize *exactly* how you placed the mugs on the table. There are several ways to do this: Mugs are best because the handles give an easy marker to look for. For example, I always place the mugs so the handle is pointed at an easy-to-find mark on the table, like a scratch or a knot in the wood. If there's a newspaper on the table, place the mug so the handle points toward a photo or headline you remember. Just don't angle the handles *all* the same way. *Note:* If you perform this onstage, you can be bolder. Make a small dot on the edge of the mug and another small dot on the table, as shown. Then, line up the dots before you start.

SECRET STUFF

Some participants might ignore your directions and not place the candy under any mug (this happens more if you try the effect twice). So if you observe that every mug is exactly how you placed it, you can amaze everyone in the room by turning to the participant and saying, *"Hey there, I thought I told you to place the candy under the mug. I don't think you listened. I sense you still have it!"* That will really surprise everyone, especially the participant.

21: HANDY CANDY

3

Say, *"I like candy. A lot. I mean, I REALLY like candy. And to show you just how much I like it, I will allow you to hide this piece of candy under any one of these three mugs. I'll leave the room while you're hiding it. When you have placed it under any mug, call me back in."* Leave the room and allow the participant to follow your instructions.

4

When you return, don't look at the mugs too carefully or someone could figure out the secret. Instead, misdirect their attention by holding your hands above each mug, as if you're "feeling" for where the candy could be. Imagine the candy gives off some kind of energy, and that you can *feel* that energy with your magic powers.

5

Walk past each mug, even if you notice the one the participant chose. After you have examined each one, return to the one she chose and say, *"I sense the candy is here."*

6

Lift up the mug, show the candy, and . . .

7

. . . eat it as your reward!

SILLY BILLY IS an expert magician when it comes to performing for kids. He should be—he has performed his show more than 10,000 times for a total of more than 300,000 children. If I could be a kid all over again, he is the guy I would want performing at my party. Since you're a kid, it's very likely that your audiences will be mostly kids, too. If I could ask one guy for advice on entertaining for kids, it would be Silly Billy. So I did!

JJ: WHAT DO YOU DO IF KIDS SHOUT OUT THINGS DURING YOUR SHOW?

SB: Sometimes children in your audience will yell out how they think you are doing your effects. They don't realize that the fun of a magic show is not to figure out the effects, but to be entertained and amazed. When you hear this, try not to be shaken by it. Instead say, "That is one way I could do this effect, but that's not how I am doing it now" (even if it *is* how you are doing it!).

JJ: HOW DO YOU KEEP THE KIDS INTERESTED DURING YOUR SHOW?

SB: Part of your magic show is fooling the audience, but you should also try to entertain them in other ways. The most common way is to make the effect funny, too. So look around your house and find things that would be funny in your magic show. Instead of using a magic wand, you can use an egg beater or a toothbrush.

JJ: GIVE US A TIP TO MAKE OUR NEXT SHOW BETTER.

SB: To be your best, there should be no distractions for the audience. Make sure that pets are in another room and that if people want to talk while you perform, that they do so *outside* the room you are performing in. And, of course, remember to have fun yourself!

BOXED IN

You display an empty box with holes punched into the sides. You help your partner into the box and then, one by one, stick nine poles through the holes. As each pole goes through the box, the mystery deepens . . . how can she fit into the box with all those poles in the way? Yet somehow, once you remove all the poles, she emerges from the box, unharmed . . . even smiling!

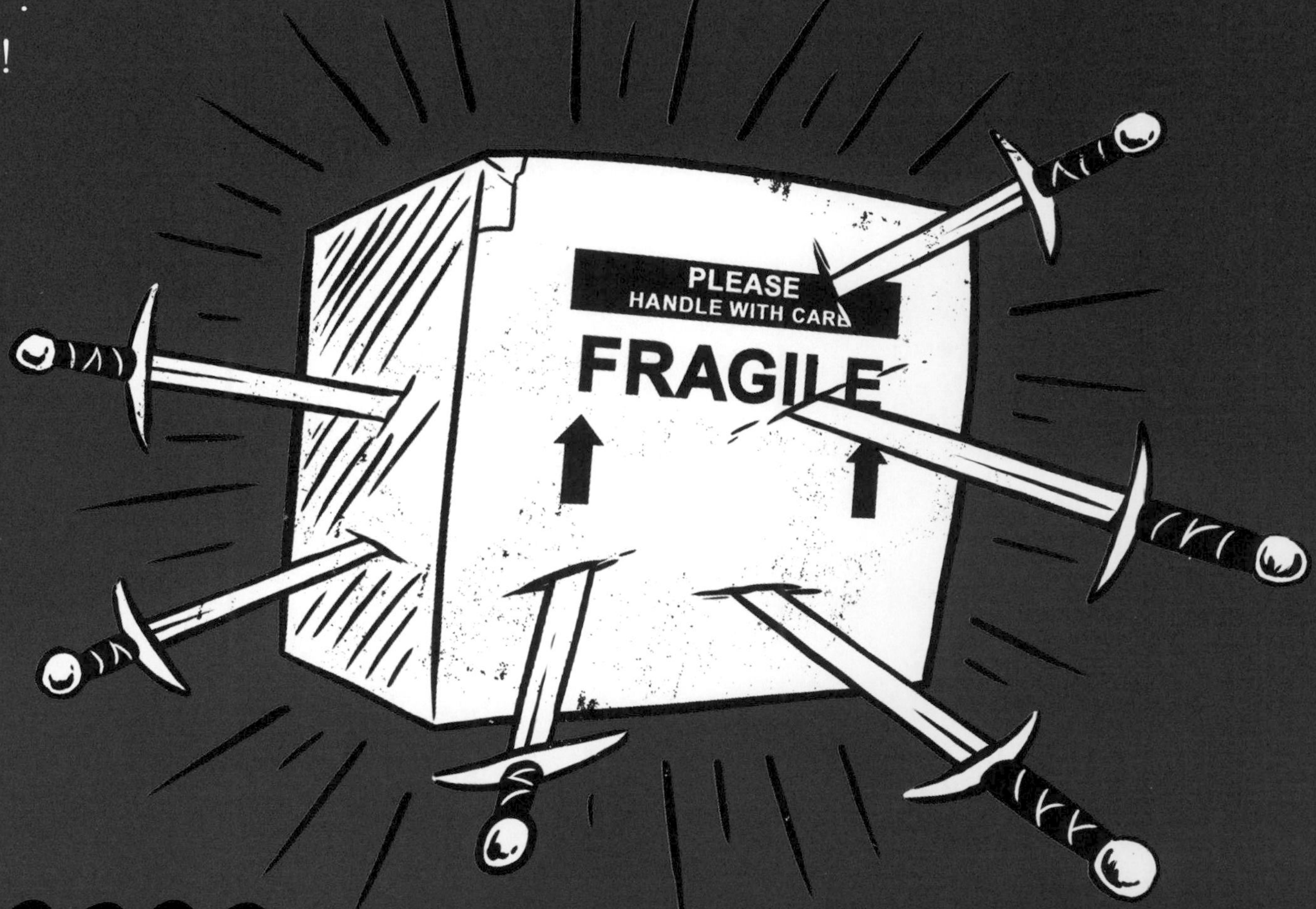

HOW IT WORKS

IN THIS CASE THE BOX LOOKS LIKE THE POLES PASS THROUGH EVERY PART OF THE INSIDE SPACE, BUT THERE IS *JUST* ENOUGH ROOM FOR A TRAINED PARTNER TO REMAIN UNHARMED.

What You Need

- A BIG BOX
  The size of this box depends entirely on the size of your partner. Your partner must be able to fit inside the box cross-legged without his or her head protruding too much. The box should have a removable lid. If your box has flaps, you can make it work, or you can take the time to fashion your own lid.
- A PENCIL
- A CRAFT KNIFE
  Ask an adult to help you poke holes in the box in just the right locations.
- NINE POLES
  The ends should be blunt or rounded—leave the sharp swords to the professionals. Broomsticks or mop handles work well, and so do yardsticks. Not every pole has to match. Be creative: think tree branches, plastic piping, poster holders, and so on.
- MUSIC

1 SETUP

Prepare the box with your partner nearby, so you can plan out the best places for the holes according to her flexibility and size. The idea is for her to position as much of her body as possible near the corners and bottom of the box, leaving the middle space open (because that is where most people expect her to be).

2

Once your partner is in position, mark the places for the poles to pass through with a pencil. Once she is outside the box, have an adult cut out the holes with a craft knife so the poles go in at various angles: Some can go in more or less straight, and others can angle up and down. Plan for three poles to go from one side to the opposite side.

3

Plan for the next three poles to pass from one of the remaining two sides to its opposite side.

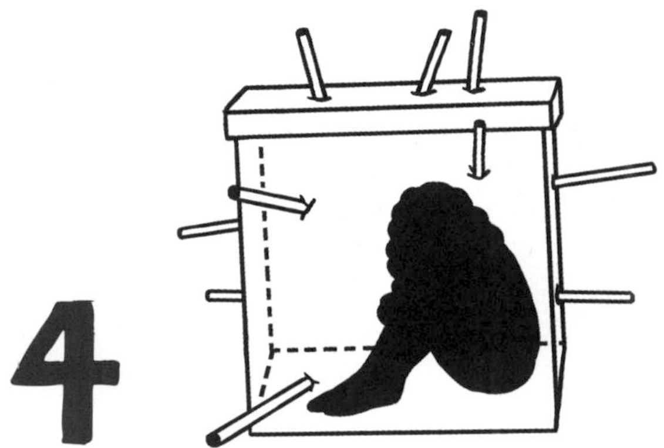

4

Finally, poke three holes in the lid so you can pass poles directly downward. This is trickier (but not impossible) if you have flaps instead of a lid. Practice this illusion by having your partner climb inside and quickly and smoothly inserting each pole into its proper place. Although the audience won't know this, she can often help you line up the poles to the proper holes from inside. Make sure that when all nine poles are in the box, she has enough room. She won't be comfortable, but she should fit. (If she doesn't, you need a bigger box or a smaller partner!)

5 PERFORMANCE

Situate the box onstage with the poles in a pile nearby. Have your partner waiting in the wings. Once your music is rolling, walk out and remove the lid. Show both sides of it and then tip the box forward so the audience can see clearly inside. Empty.

6

Invite your partner onstage. Help her into the box and then replace the lid. Once out of sight, she must get into the rehearsed position so she will be out of the way of the poles.

7

Then, just like you rehearsed, begin poking the box with the poles. Start slowly, and then move faster and faster. This illusion gets more impressive with every pole you push through the box. When all nine poles are through, take a bow.

TEAMWORK

Magicians become famous for being singular, fascinating people: Harry Houdini, Harry Blackstone, David Copperfield. But like the illusion you just learned, it always takes a great *team* of people to make magic work.

For example, Houdini's wife, Bess, assisted him in his shows for most of his career. And by most accounts, she was fantastic at her job. Siegfried and Roy combined their talents to become a magical duo. Harry Blackstone was one of magic's most recognizable faces, yet he traveled with a crew of *forty* people. Everyone worked together to create one of the greatest shows in magic.

Even when you perform alone, you're really a team. I'm on your team, supplying you with some amazing illusions. Whoever helps build your props is part of your team, too. Your partners are a big part of the team. And if Mom and Dad help give advice, they become your directors. So when we think of magicians, we think of the guy in the top hat waving the wand. But the big secret of magic is cooperation.

8

Now remove the poles quickly and throw them back into a pile, one by one. Remove the lid and throw it dramatically offstage. As you do this, your partner crawls back to her knees, ready to spring up. Then clap your hands and she *jumps* to a standing position, arms in the air, to receive a big round of applause for a job well done.

SECRET STUFF

To add one final amazing moment, you may want to include a costume change. To do this, your partner has to have two costumes on, in contrasting colors. The first one must be hidden under the second one. And, your partner must practice getting the outside layer off quickly. She will have to do it in two steps: She has a few seconds when she first enters the box but before there are too many poles in her way, and she has a little more time at the end, as the last pole is coming out.

WONDER-MINT

You show a tin with mints of all different colors: blue, red, yellow, green, and orange—or any combination. You pour all the mints into a participant's cupped hands and ask him to close them and think of any one color—perhaps the green mints. When he opens his hands, he discovers that ALL the mints have changed to green. Then you can invite him to take one and pass out the rest to the other participants.

HOW IT WORKS

IT'S A GAFFED TIN. ALL THE MINTS ARE GLUED INTO PLACE EXCEPT THE GREEN MINTS.

What You Need

- ☞ GLUE
  You need a kind that dries clear.
- ☞ MINTS OF VARIOUS COLORS
  I use Tic Tacs, but you could also use any colored candy. Four or five colors work best. (Make sure one of the colors is green.)
- ☞ A SMALL TIN CONTAINER WITH LID
  Many mints come in a container like this, or a parent probably has a spare one, if you ask nicely. The tin should be small enough that you can turn it over and dump out the contents into someone's cupped hands.

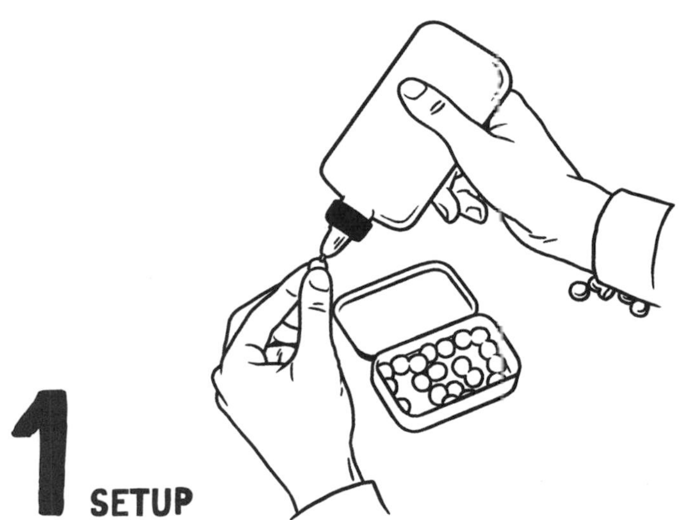

1 SETUP

Glue twenty mints to the bottom of the container: reds, blues, yellows . . . just not any green mints. (Set those aside for now.) Allow the glued mints to dry in place.

2

Now dump the green mints into the container. It looks like an assortment of colors, but if you turn the container upside down, only the green mints fall out. This is how the effect works. Snap the lid closed and you're ready.

3 PERFORMANCE

Invite a participant onstage to help you, or gather a crowd if you're performing impromptu. Say, *"There are several colors of mints in this tin. Can you name them all?"* Remove the lid and allow someone to look inside and list off all the colors. Then walk around so that the other audience members can see all the different colors.

4

Ask the participant to cup her hands together. Dump the mints into her hands by turning the container upside down. Ask her to make a fist around all the mints.

5

Wait until her hands are closed before you move the container away. Place the lid on the container, being careful not to flash the glued mints at the bottom of the can. Put the container away. You're done with it.

6

Ask the participant, *"What is your favorite color?"* If she answers green, you're set. If she answers anything other than green, just shrug and say, *"Interesting. Well, my favorite is green. So let me show you what I do with all the other mints."* Either way, you finish the effect the same way: *"I will cause all the other colors to change into green."* Snap your fingers and allow her to open her hands, where she will discover only green mints. Invite her to pop one in her mouth and share the rest with the other participants.

SECRET STUFF

You might wonder whether this would really fool people. *"Won't they notice there are fewer mints at the end of the effect than there were at the beginning?"*

The answer is no. No, they won't notice. Unless you say, *"Please count how many mints are in this container,"* nobody will count. Instead, you ask them to focus on the colors of the mints. Audience members can only focus on one or two details at a time. One of the key principles in magic is never to allow the audience to focus on the right details.

CRAYON CONJURING

Even if presented with a full box—an astonishing array of sixty-four colors—you are able to tell the color of a single crayon . . . just by feel!

HOW IT WORKS

YOU SECRETLY SNEAK A LITTLE CRAYON WAX UNDER YOUR THUMBNAIL SO YOU CAN SNEAK A PEEK, EVEN WHEN THE CRAYON IS NO LONGER IN YOUR HANDS.

What You Need

- ☞ BOX OF CRAYONS
- ☞ CLOTH NAPKIN

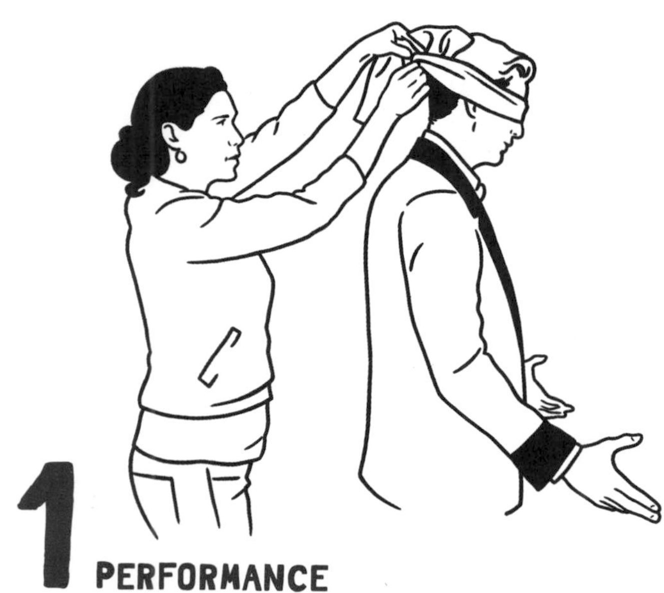

1 PERFORMANCE

Borrow a set of crayons from a friend and gather a crowd. Ask someone to tie the cloth napkin around your head so your eyes are covered.

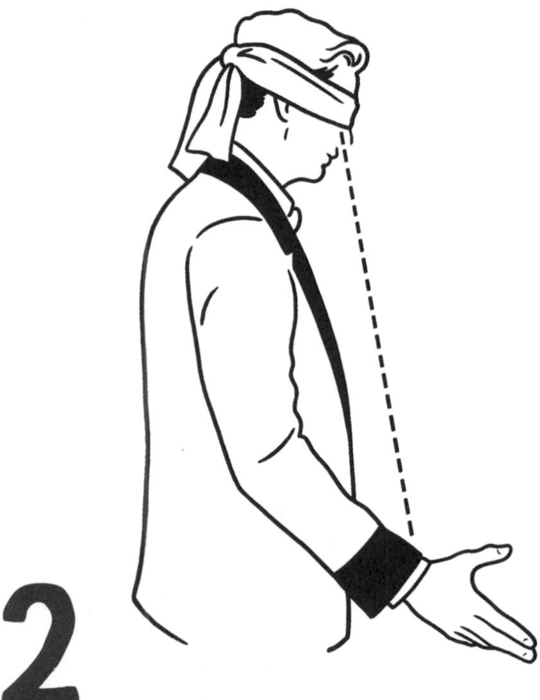

2

From all angles, it looks like you can't see a thing. But, actually, you can still see! If you look straight down, you can see quite well.

3

Start by instructing a volunteer: *"Please open the crayon box and take out any color. Most people look with their eyes, but I can see with my fingertips. Please hand me the crayon behind my back and I'll feel for the color."* So saying, place both hands behind your back and ask the participant to hand you a crayon.

HIDDEN VIEW

4

Step back a few steps so that nobody can see behind your back. Scrape your thumb against one end of the crayon so a small flake of crayon wax goes under your nail.

What You Need

- ☞ WHITE CONFETTI
  Magic shops carry white circular confetti, and it's sort of expensive. But there are endless amounts of free confetti waiting for you at school, in the bottom tray of the three-hole punch. Just use that, or punch your own from paper.
- ☞ TWO WHITE PAPER NAPKINS
- ☞ A RUBBER BAND
- ☞ SCISSORS
- ☞ A BOWL FILLED WITH WATER
  It doesn't have to be a big bowl but it must not be see-through.
- ☞ A FAN
  You can make your own out of stiff paper or use a slick, collapsible one.
- ☞ MUSIC

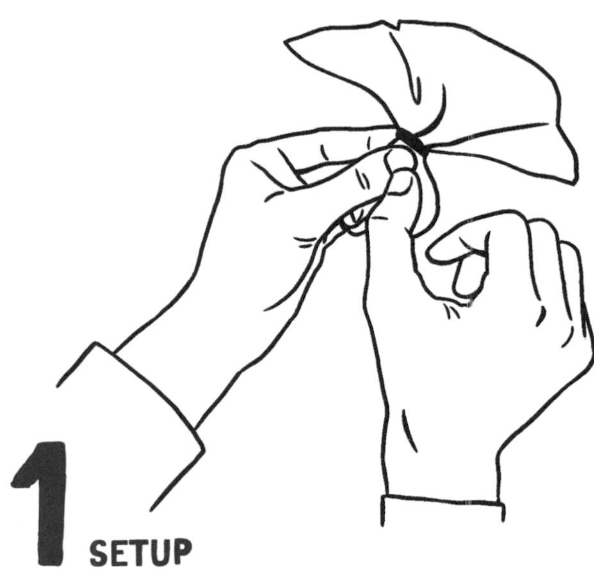

1 SETUP

First, set up the secret confetti packet: Fill a napkin with confetti and then seal it closed by wrapping the ends with a rubber band.

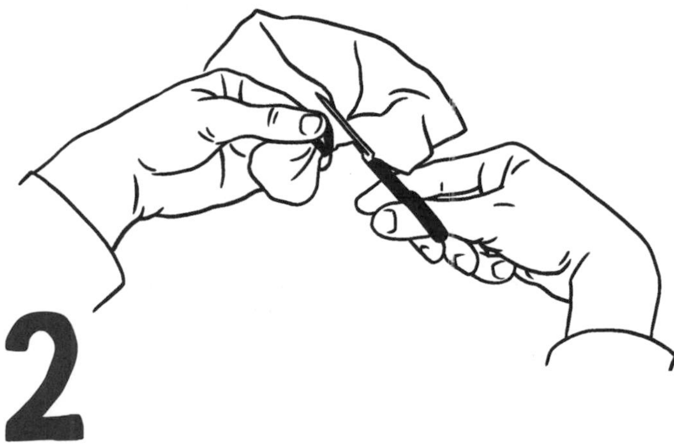

2

Use scissors to trim off the extra napkin's ends. The packet should fit comfortably in your hand and not show when your fingers are wrapped around it.

3

Place the trimmed packet on the table *behind* the water bowl. From the front, your audience shouldn't be able to see it. Place the fan and the unprepared napkin behind the bowl, where you can grab them easily.

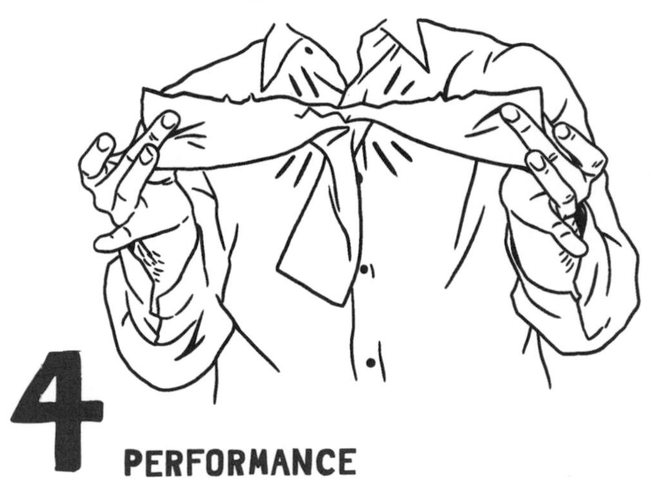

4 PERFORMANCE

Say, *"My favorite season of the year is winter. So when it's hot out, I have to do magic to make it snow. Like this . . ."* Cue the music to start. Retrieve the napkin and tear it into small strips.

5

Wad the napkin pieces into a ball in your left hand and approach your table from the left side.

6

As you dunk the napkin pieces into the water, casually place your right hand behind the bowl and wrap your fingers around the confetti packet.

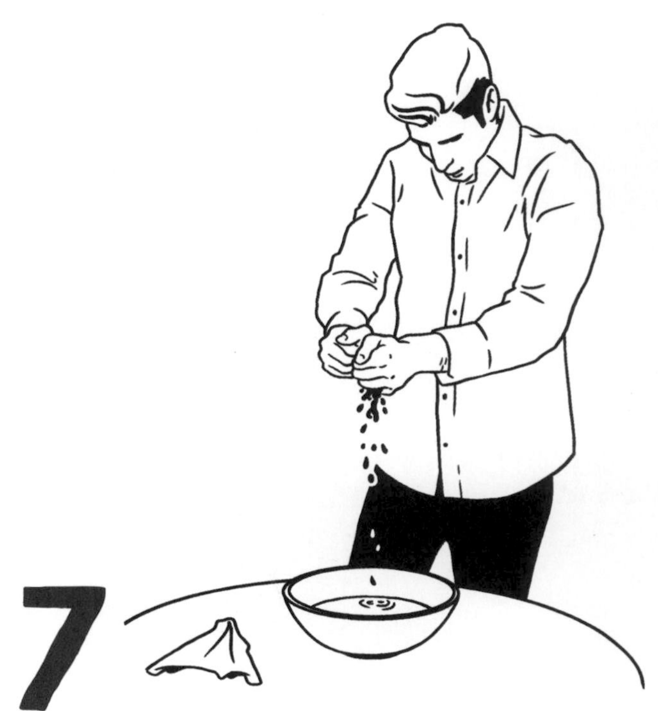

7

Lift both hands at the same time and apparently wring out the water from the napkin with both hands. Actually, you put your fists together, but keep the contents of both hands separate.

8

Push the confetti packet up to your right fingertips and display it to the audience as you move your left hand behind the bowl.

HIDDEN VIEW

With your left hand, secretly drop the wet napkin ball behind the bowl, out of sight, as you pick up the fan.

Wave the fan as quickly as you can toward your right hand as you walk forward, near the front of the stage. As you do this, massage the confetti packet in your right hand, tearing the napkin open.

This movement allows the confetti to get lifted by the wind of the fan, causing it to create a snowstorm all around your body. It looks like a snow globe from a distance. When the confetti is more or less gone from the packet, simply let go of the whole thing. The torn napkin packet will float a bit in the air and then fall, blending in with all the other white confetti.

SECRET STUFF

This is one to perform only onstage. If you perform it inside, your parents will be finding confetti well into your high school years, and you just might be grounded until that time.

Ignore Me, PLEASE

I WAS SEVEN when I became interested in magic but there was a big problem: There were no magic schools or magic shops nearby. I was able to read some books and order some effects, but I didn't have anyone to tell me what to *say* when I performed. I had to just make it all up. And you know what? That was a good thing.

Why? Figuring out what to say during a magic effect is important. Your words can make an effect silly or serious, and your words are what make the effects your own. Master magicians always use their own words, and speak from their hearts. I have given you some suggestions of what you can say while you perform each effect, always in italics, *like this*. But feel free to ignore the words I suggest. Believe me, I won't mind. In fact, I'll be happy because if you use your creativity to develop your own words and presentation, you will be on your way to becoming a true master magician.

This book is full of amazing magic effects. But more than that, this book is full of *possibilities*. As soon as you learn the routines, change them. Once you understand the rules of magic, feel free to break them. All the great magicians do.

Conclusion

The Big Finale

BY NOW I HOPE YOU HAVE BUILT PROPS, rehearsed effects, and most importantly, felt the thrill of making magic. Sometimes people ask me, "Is there such a thing as real magic?" I don't know the answer to that question, but I do know this: The closest thing to feeling *real* magic is performing for people, and helping them experience the impossible.

I'm guessing this is your first magic book, but I hope it won't be your last. Here are some ideas for your next magical adventure:

***Under, Over*:** This is a *free* ebook I wrote for kids (those *under* 18) and their parents (those *over* 18). This contains advice, effects, and more if you're serious about performing magic at parties. You can get it for free at vanishingincmagic.com.

THE COMPLETE MAGICIAN: This is a great beginner's magic kit with special props: a Pen through Bill effect, a special deck of cards, Linking Rings, and more.

MAGIC: The Complete Course: I wrote this introduction to magic for all ages, but there are plenty of great effects here for kids, too. The coolest part? It comes with a DVD of me performing and teaching some of my favorite effects.

Society of Young Magicians: Get this—there are young magicians' clubs, where kids just like you meet to learn, perform, and talk magic. Visit magicsam.com for details.

Credits

Your First Magical Moment Parts of this introduction were inspired by my own *Under, Over.*

Levitating Your Brother (or Sister) When I was seven years old, I read a similar effect in *The Klutz Book of Magic*, and the basic illusion is at least 200 years old. I made alterations to make it easier to perform with stuff found around the house, and to improve the look of the illusion.

Magic Pitcher Louis Nikola is often considered the creator of this classic effect, though Okito and Richard Himber's advancements are critical to the illusion as it is described here.

Knot Just Imagination was invented by Pavel, the great Swiss magician, and it is my favorite effect from this book to perform. Pavel passed away in 2011, but his family was gracious enough to allow its inclusion here. It was originally called "Pavel's Blow Knot" (*Tarbell Course in Magic*, vol. 7, p. 374).

It's a Wrap is based on much older illusions, but this particular sequence was performed by Dante (Harry Jansen), a famous magician who toured the world in the 1940s.

Spook-Key was popularized by the great Dr. Jaks, but its origin, sometime before 1900, is unknown.

Rope Escape is essentially an escape method popularized by Harry Kellar and used even by the great Harry Houdini.

Egg-straordinary was invented by Joe Karson, who created some of the most memorable stage magic of the last century.

Thumbthing Cool is a great impromptu illusion that is old and uncredited, but the idea of stretching the thumb between the teeth comes from the modern master of fingertip illusions, my friend Meir Yedid (see "The Elongated Thumb," *Finger Secrets*, 1985).

Hat Trick is inspired by "It's a Hat, So It's Funny, Right?" by Charles Hardin (in *Penn & Teller's How to Play in Traffic*). This article proposed a similar concept but as a prank to get someone to walk out of a hat shop wearing a hat he or she didn't pay for.

Orna-Mental originally appeared in the November 2008 issue of *MAGIC Magazine*. I devised it so I could perform an effect at my girlfriend's parents' house on Christmas Eve. I knew I needed something strong and yet thematic for the holiday. My friend Raj Madhok came up with the second part, which really makes the effect great.

Notebook of Secrets is based on a very, very old principle called the "Blow Book" that dates back at least to the 1500s.

Traveling Juice is based on "Sprightly Soda" from Karl Fulves's *Self-Working Paper Magic*, p. 87. Fulves attributes the basic concept to Sam Berland.

Sponge Swindle falls under the category of Sponge Ball magic. In 1926, Jesse Lybarger and Joe Berg may have been some of the earliest magicians to develop magic with sponges, and all modern sponge magic owes a debt to Albert Goshman, who manufactured and innovated with sponge balls.

Handy Candy is a fun variation of Al Koran's "Note Under Cup."

Boxed In is based on the classic Indian "Sword Basket" illusion. No originator is known. Hans Moretti, a popular escape artist, performed a marvelous illusion that is similar in effect.